Franklin's Way to Wealth & Penn's Maxims

Benjamin Franklin
William Penn

"Industry leads to wealth
Piety to heaven."

DOVER PUBLICATIONS, INC.
Mineola, New York

Bibliographical Note

This Dover edition, first published in 2008, is a republication of the work originally published in 1837 by Daniel & Geo. F. Cooledge, Booksellers, New York.

Library of Congress Cataloging-in-Publication Data

Franklin, Benjamin, 1706–1790.
    Franklin's Way to wealth; and, Penn's maxims / Benjamin Franklin, William Penn.
    Reprint. Originally published: New York : Daniel & Geo. F. Cooledge, 1837.
      p. cm.
    Penn, William, 1644–1718. Some fruits of solitude, in reflections and maxims relating to the conduct of human life.
    ISBN-13: 978-0-486-45460-3 (pbk.)
    ISBN-10: 0-486-45460-6 (pbk.)
    1. Wealth—Quotations, maxims, etc. 2. Success—Quotations, maxims, etc. 3. Saving and investment. 4. Conduct of life—Early works to 1800. 5. Maxims, American.

HF5386.F6 2007
332.024/01 22

2006050283

Manufactured in the United States by Courier Corporation
45460602   2014
www.doverpublications.com

FRANKLIN'S

WAY TO WEALTH

Introduction

This little treatise is much and justly admired, as well as its celebrated and ingenious author; in short, it is to be doubted whether any other work of the kind equal to it ever appeared. It has been repeatedly published, in different sizes; and made its appearance on both sides of the Atlantic. The London copy, from which this is printed, contains the following introduction:

"Dr. Franklin, wishing to collect into one piece all the sayings upon the following subjects, which he had dropped in the course of publishing the Almanac, called 'Poor Richard,' introduces Father Abraham for this purpose. Hence it is that Poor Richard is so often quoted, and that in the present title he is said to be improved. Notwithstanding the stroke of humor in the concluding paragraph of this address, Poor Richard Saunders and Father Abraham have proved, in America, that they are no common preachers; and shall we, brother Englishmen, refuse good sense and saving knowledge, because it comes from the other side of the water?"

Courteous Reader,—

I have heard that nothing gives an author so great pleasure, as to find his works respectfully quoted by others. Judge, then, how much I must have been gratified by an incident I am going to relate to you. I stopped my horse, lately, where a great number of people were collected at an auction of merchants' goods. The hour of the sale not being come, they were conversing on the badness of the times; and one of the company called to a plain, clean old man, with white locks, "Pray, Father Abraham, what think you of the times? Will not these heavy taxes quite ruin the country? How shall we ever be able to pay them? What would you advise us to?" Father Abraham stood up, and replied, "If you would have my advice, I will give it you in short, for 'a word to the wise is enough,' as Poor Richard says." They joined in desiring him to speak his mind, and, gathering around him, he proceeded as follows:—

"Friends," said he, "the taxes are indeed very heavy; and if those laid on by the government were the only ones we had to pay, we might more easily discharge them; but we have many others, and much more grievous to some of us. We are taxed twice as much by our idleness, three times as much by our pride, and four times as much by our folly; and from these taxes the commissioners cannot ease or deliver us, by allowing an abatement. However, let us hearken to good advice, and something may be done for us. 'God helps them that help themselves,' as Poor Richard says.

"I. It would be thought a hard government that should tax its people one-tenth part of their time to be employed in its service; but idleness taxes many of us much more. Sloth, by bringing on diseases, absolutely shortens life.

"'Sloth, like rust, consumes faster than labor wears; while the used key is always bright,' as Poor Richard says. 'But dost thou love life? then do not squander time for that is the stuff life is made of,' as Poor Richard says. How much more than is necessary do we spend in sleep! forgetting that 'the sleeping fox catches no poultry, and that there will be sleeping enough in the grave,' as Poor Richard says.

"If time be of all things the most precious, 'wasting time must be,' as Poor Richard says, 'the greatest prodigality!' since, as he elsewhere tells us, 'Lost time is never found again; and what we call time enough, always proves little enough.' Let us, then, up and be doing, and doing to the purpose; so, by diligence, shall we do more with less perplexity. 'Sloth makes all things difficult, but industry all easy; and he that riseth late must trot all day, and shall scarce overtake his business at night; while laziness travels so slowly, that poverty soon overtakes him. Drive thy business, let not that drive thee; and early to bed, and early to rise, makes a man healthy, wealthy, and wise,' as Poor Richard says.

"So what signify wishing and hoping for better times? We may make these times better, if we bestir ourselves. 'Industry need not wish, and he that lives upon hope will die fasting. There are no gains without pains; then, help hands, for I have no lands;' or, if I have, they are smartly taxed. 'He that hath a trade, hath an estate; and he that hath a calling, hath an office of profit and honor,' as Poor Richard says. But then the trade must be worked at, and the calling well followed, or neither the estate nor the office will enable us to pay our taxes. If we are industrious, we shall never starve; for, 'at the working man's house hunger looks in, but dares not enter.' Nor will the bailiff or constable enter; for 'industry pays debts, while despair increaseth them.' What enough you have found no treasure, nor has any rich relation left you a legacy; 'Diligence is the mother of good luck, and God gives all things to industry. Then plough deep, while sluggards sleep, and you shall have corn to sell and to keep.' Work while it is called to-day, for you know not how much you may be hindered to-morrow. 'One to-day is worth two to-morrows,' as Poor

Richard says; and farther, 'Never leave that till to-morrow which you can do to-day.' If you were a servant, would you not be ashamed that a good master should catch you idle? Are you, then, your own master? Be ashamed to catch yourself idle, when there is so much to be done for yourself, your family, your country, and benevolent movements. Handle your tools without mittens; remember that 'The cat in gloves catches no mice,' as Poor Richard says. It is true, there is much to be done; and, perhaps, you are weak-handed: but stick to it steadily, and you will see great effects; for 'Constant dropping wears away stone; and by diligence and patience the mouse ate in two the cable; and little strokes fell great oaks.'

"Methinks I hear some of you say, 'Must a man afford himself no leisure?' I will tell thee, my friend, what Poor Richard says: 'Employ thy time well, if thou meanest to gain leisure; and since thou art not sure of a minute, throw not away an hour.' Leisure is time for doing something useful: this leisure the diligent man will obtain, but the lazy man never; for 'A life of leisure and a life of laziness are two things. Many, without labor, would live by their wits only; but they break for want of stock:' whereas, industry gives comfort, and plenty, and respect. 'Fly pleasures, and they will follow you. The diligent spinner has a large shift; and now I have a sheep and a cow, everybody bids me good morrow.'

"II. But with our industry we must likewise be steady, settled, and careful, and oversee our own affairs with our own eyes, and not trust too much to others; for, as Poor Richard says:—

> 'I never saw an oft-removed tree,
> Nor yet an oft-removed family,
> That throve so well as those that settled be.'

And again, 'Three removes are as bad as a fire:' and again, 'Keep thy shop, and thy shop will keep thee:' and again, 'If you would have your business done, go; if not, send:' And again,

> 'He that by the plough would thrive,
> Himself must either hold or drive.'

And again, 'The eye of the master will do more work than both his hands:' and again, 'Want of care does us more damage than want of knowledge:' and again, 'Not to oversee workmen, is to leave them your purse open.'

"Trusting too much to others' care is the ruin of many; for, 'In the affairs of this world, men are saved, not by faith, but by the want of it. But a man's own care is profitable; for if you would have a faithful servant, and one that you like, serve yourself. A little neglect may breed great mischief; for want of a nail, the shoe was lost; for want of a shoe, the horse was lost; and for want of a horse, the rider was lost;' being overtaken and slain by the enemy, all for want of a little care about a horse-shoe nail.

"III. So much for industry, my friends, and attention to one's own business; but to these we must add frugality, if we would make our industry more certainly successful. A man may, if he know not how to save as he gets, 'keep his nose all his life to the grindstone, and die not worth a groat at last. A fat kitchen makes a lean will;' and

> 'Many estates are spent in getting,
> Since women for tea forsook spinning and knitting,
> And men for punch forsook hewing and splitting.'

'If you would be wealthy, think of saving as well as of getting. The Indies have not made Spain rich, because her outgoes are greater than her incomes.'

"Away, then, with your expensive follies, and you will not then have so much cause to complain of hard times, heavy taxes, and chargeable families; for,

> 'Women and wine, game and deceit,
> Make the wealth small, and the want great.'

And farther, 'What maintains one vice would bring up two children.' You may think, perhaps, that a little tea, or a little punch now and then, diet a little more costly, clothes a little finer, and a little entertainment now and then, can be no great matter; but remember, 'Many a little make a mickle.' Beware of little expenses; 'A small leak will sink a great ship,' as Poor Richard says: and again, 'Who dainties love, shall beggars prove;' and moreover, 'Fools make feasts, and wise men eat them.' Here you are all got together to this sale of fineries and nic-nacs. You call them goods; but, if you do not take care, they will prove evils to some of you. You expect they will be sold cheap, and, perhaps, they may for less than they cost: but if you have no occasion for them, they may be dear to you. Remember what Poor Richard says, 'Buy what thou hast no need of, and ere long thou shalt sell thy necessaries.' And again, 'At a great pennyworth pause awhile'; he means, that perhaps the cheapness is apparent only, and not real; or the bargain, by straitening thee in thy business, may do thee more harm than good: for in another place he says, 'Many have been ruined by buying good pennyworths.' Again, 'It is foolish to lay out money in a purchase of repentance;' and yet this folly is practised every day at auctions, for want of minding the Almanac. Many a one, for the sake of finery on the back, has gone with a hungry belly, and half starved his family. 'Silks and satins, scarlet and velvets, put out the kitchen fire,' as Poor Richard says. These are not the necessaries of life; they can scarcely be called the conveniences; and yet, only because they look pretty, how many want to have them! By these and other extravagances, the genteel are reduced to poverty, and forced to borrow of those whom they formerly despised, but who, through industry and frugality, have maintained their standing; in which case it appears plainly, that 'A ploughman on his legs is higher than a gentleman on his knees,' as Poor Richard says. Perhaps they have had a small estate left them, which they knew not the getting of; they think 'it is day, and will never be night;' that a little to be spent out of so much is not worth minding; but, 'Always taking out of the meal-tub, and never putting in, soon comes to the bottom,' as Poor Richard says: and then, 'when the well is dry, they know the worth of water.' But this they might have known before, if they had taken his advice. 'If you would know the value of money, go and try to borrow some; for he that goes a borrowing, goes a sorrowing,' as Poor Richard says; and, indeed, so does he that lends to such people, when he goes to get it in again. Poor Dick farther advises, and says,

> 'Fond pride of dress is sure a very curse:
> Ere fancy you consult, consult your purse.'

And again, 'Pride is as loud a beggar as Want, and a great deal more saucy.' When you have bought one fine thing, you must buy ten more, that your appearance may be all of a piece; but Poor Dick says, 'It is easier to suppress the first desire, than to satisfy all that follow it. And it is as truly folly for the poor to ape the rich, as for the frog to swell, in order to equal the ox.'

> 'Vessels large may venture more,
> But little boats should keep near shore.'

"It is, however, a folly soon punished; for, as Poor Richard says, 'Pride, that dines on vanity, sups on contempt. Pride breakfasted with Plenty, dined with Poverty, and supped with Infamy.' And, after all, of what use is this pride of appearance, for which so much is risked, so much is suffered? It cannot promote health, nor ease pain; it makes no increase of merit in the person, it creates envy, it hastens misfortune.

"But what madness it must be to run in debt for these superfluities! We are offered, by the terms of this sale, six months credit; and that, perhaps, has induced some of us to attend it, because we cannot spare the ready money, and hope now to be fine without it. But, ah! think what you do when you run in debt: you give to another power over your liberty. If you cannot pay at the time, you will be ashamed to see your creditor; you will be in fear when you speak to him; you will make poor, pitiful, sneaking excuses; and, by degrees, come to lose your veracity, and sink into base downright lying; for, 'The second vice is lying, the first is running in debt,' as Poor Richard says;' and again, to the same purpose, 'Lying rides upon Debt's back:' whereas a freeborn man ought not to be ashamed or afraid to see or speak to any man living. But poverty often deprives a man of all spirit and virtue. 'It is hard for an empty bag to stand upright.' What would you think of that prince, or of that government, who should issue an edict forbidding you to dress like a gentleman or gentlewoman, on pain of imprisonment or servitude? Would not you say you are free, have a right to dress as you please, and that such an edict would be a breach of your privileges, and such a government tyrannical? And yet you are about to put yourself under that tyranny, when you run in debt for such dress! Your creditor has authority, at his pleasure, to deprive you of your liberty, by confining you in jail for life, or by selling you for a servant, if you should not be able to pay him. When you have got your bargain, you may, perhaps, think little of payment; but, as Poor Richard says, 'Creditors have better memories than debtors; creditors are a superstitious sect, great observers of set days and times.' The day comes round before you are aware, and the demand is made before you are prepared to satisfy it; or, if you bear your debt in mind, the term, which at first seemed so long, will, as it lessens, appear extremely short: Time will seem to have added wings to his heels as well as his shoulders. 'Those have a short Lent, who owe money to be paid at Easter.' At present, perhaps, you may think yourselves in thriving circumstances, and that you can bear a little extravagance without injury; but,

'For age and want save while you may:
No morning sun lasts a whole day.'

"Gain may be temporary and uncertain; but ever, while you live, expense is constant and certain; and 'It is easier to build two chimneys, than to keep one in fuel,' as Poor Richard says; so 'Rather go to bed supperless, than rise in debt.'

'Get what you can, and what you get hold;
'Tis the stone that will turn all your lead into gold.'

And when you have got the philosopher's stone, sure you will no longer complain of bad times, or of the difficulty of paying taxes.

"IV. This doctrine, my friends, is reason and wisdom; but, after all, do not depend too much upon your own industry, and frugality, and prudence, though excellent things; for they may all be blasted, without the blessing of Heaven; and, therefore, ask that blessing humbly, and be not uncharitable to those that at present seem to want it, but comfort and help them. Remember, Job suffered, and was afterwards prosperous.

"And now, to conclude: 'Experience keeps a dear school, but fools will learn in no other,' as Poor Richard says, and scarce in that; for it is true, 'We may give advice, but we cannot give conduct.' However, remember this, 'They that will not be counselled, cannot be helped;' and further, 'If you will not hear

Reason, she will surely rap your knuckles,' as Poor Richard says."

Thus the old gentleman ended his harangue. The people heard it, and approved the doctrine, and immediately practised the contrary, just as if it had been a common sermon; for the auction opened, and they began to buy extravagantly. I found the good man had thoroughly studied my Almanacs, and digested all I had dropped on those topics during the course of twenty-five years. The frequent mention he made of me must have tired any one else; but my vanity was wonderfully delighted with it, though I was conscious that not a tenth part of the wisdom was my own, which he ascribed to me; but rather the gleanings that I had made of the sense of all ages and nations. However, I resolved to be the better for the echo of it; and though I had at first determined to buy stuff for a new coat, I went away, resolved to wear my old one a little longer. Reader, if thou wilt do the same, thy profit will be as great as mine. I am, as ever, thine to serve thee,

RICHARD SAUNDERS.

ADVICE TO A YOUNG TRADESMAN
FROM
AN OLD ONE.
BY DR. BENJAMIN FRANKLIN

REMEMBER that time is money. He that can earn 10s. a day by his labor, and goes abroad or sits idle one-half of that day, though he spend but 6d. during his diversion or idleness, ought not to reckon that the only expense; he has really spent, or rather thrown away, 5s. besides.

Remember that credit is money. If a man lets money lie in my hands after it is due, he gives me the interest, or so much as I can make of it during that time. This amounts to a considerable sum, if a man has a good and large credit, and makes good use of it.

Remember that money is of a prolific, generating nature. Money can beget money, and its offspring can beget more, and so on; 5s. turned, is 6s., turned again, is 7s. 3d.; and so on till it becomes 100l. The more there is of it, the more it produces every turning; so that the profits rise quicker and quicker. He that kills a breeding sow, destroys all her offspring to the thousandth generation. He that murders a crown, destroys all that it might have produced, even scores of pounds.

Remember that six pounds a year is but a groat a day. For this little sum, which may daily be wasted in time or expense, unperceived, a man of credit may, on his own security, have the constant use and possession of 100l. So much in stock, briskly turned by an industrious man, produces great advantage.

Remember this saying: that *the good paymaster is lord of another man's purse.* He that is known to pay punctually and exactly at the time he promises, may at any time, and on any occasion raise all the money his friends can spare. This is sometimes of great use; therefore, never keep borrowed money an hour beyond the time you promised, lest a disappointment shut up your friend's purse for ever.

The most trifling actions, that affect a man's credit, are to be regarded. The sound of your hammer at five in the morning, or nine at night, heard by a creditor, makes him easy six months longer. But if he sees you at a billiard table, or hears your voice at a tavern when you should be at work, he sends for his money the next day. Finer clothes than he or his wife wears, or greater expense in any particular than he affords himself, shocks his pride, and he duns you to humble you. Creditors are a kind of people that have the sharpest eyes and ears, as well as the best memories, of any in the world.

Good-natured creditors (and such one would always choose to deal with, if one could) feel pain when they are obliged to ask for money. Spare them that pain, and they will love you. When you receive a sum of money, divide it among them according to your debts. Do not be ashamed of paying a small sum, because you owe a greater. Money, more or less, is always welcome; and your creditor would sooner be at the trouble of receiving 10*l.* voluntarily brought him, though at ten different times or payments, than be obliged to go ten different times to demand it, before he can receive it in a lump. It shows that you are mindful of what you owe; it makes you appear a careful as well as an honest man, and that still increases your credit.

Beware of thinking all your own that you possess, and of living accordingly. It is a mistake that many people who have credit fall into. To prevent this, keep an exact account for some time of both your expenses and incomes. If you take the pains at first to mention particulars, it will have this good effect: you will discover how wonderfully small trifling expenses mount up to large sums, and will discern what might have been, and may for the future, be saved, without occasioning any great inconvenience.

In short, the way to wealth, if you desire it, is as plain as the way to market. It depends chiefly on two words—*industry* and *frugality;* that is, waste neither your time nor money, but make the best use of both. He that gets all he can, and saves all he gets, (necessary expenses excepted,) will certainly become rich; if that Being who governs the world, to whom all should look for a blessing on their honest endeavors, does not, in his wise providence, otherwise determine.

PRO BONO PUBLICO

A NEW WAY

OF

PAYING OLD DEBTS

The following letter was received by the editor of the
Leeds Mercury, from a tradesman in Huddersfield.

"Why should excuse be born, or e'er begot?"
Shakspeare.

MR. EDITOR,—

A correspondent of yours, in the Mercury of last week, has
taken some pains to instruct your readers in their *Christmas
religious duties;* permit me to make the same experiment upon
the *Christmas moral duties,* not of your readers only, for my
philanthropy is more extensive; and, on the ground of *punctual-
ity,* I wish to be the reformer of the world.

There is no talent, Sir, in the application of which some gen-
tlemen more excel, than that of *excusing;* and when I tell you
that I am a tradesman, obliged, from the nature of my business,
to give credit, I hope you will not doubt that experience has
qualified me to speak upon this subject, and to speak feelingly.

There are two kinds of *debtors:* those who *cannot* pay, and
those who *will not* pay. The former have excuses *ready made;*
the latter are *obliged* to *make* excuses. The former may be *sometimes* dishonest; the latter are never *very* honest. The former
destroy hope at one blow; the latter protract its torments, till it
expires from weakness. The former is an *acute distemper,* that
kills in a few hours; the latter is a *chronic distemper,* worse than
death. In a word, Sir, inability is tolerable, because *they* cannot
cure it; *unwillingness* is painful, because I cannot shorten it.

In *forming excuses,* according to the common practice, the
following rules are observed:—

1st. That the *same* excuse shall be as seldom repeated as possible.

2nd. That the excuses be as various and *plausible* as possible.

3d. By way of maxim: every kind and degree of excuse deserves to be tried, because there is much less inconvenience in postponing a debt, than in paying it; and the advantages of *giving words* and *parting* with *money,* are on the side of the former.

To exemplify these rules, Mr. Editor, permit me to state the case of a bill which I sent to one of my customers last new-year, (for, to be candid, the approach of that season has tempted me to trouble you on the present occasion.) Now, mark the excuses in succession.

Jan. 1. "Oh! this is Mr. L——'s bill. Call again any day next week."

Jan. 9. "Not at home."—"When will he be at home?"—"Any time to-morrow."

Jan. 10. "Has a gentleman with him."—Waits an hour.—"Oh! ah! this is the bill—ay-hem!—look in on Tuesday."

Tuesday. "Not at home—gone to the Cloth-Hall."

Thursday. "Leave the bill, and I will look it over."

20. "There seems to be a mistake in the bill: I never had *this* article. Take it back to your master, and tell him to examine his books."

24. "Just gone out."

29. "I am busy now: tell your master I'll call on him as I go into the town."

Feb. 16. "Bless me! I quite forgot to call. This bill is not discharged! Bring me a receipt any time to-morrow or next day."

17. "Gone to London, and won't be at home till next month."

March 12. "What! did not I pay that bill before I went out of town?—Are you going farther?"

"Yes."—"Very well; call as you come back, and I'll settle."—Calls, and he is gone to dinner at Holmfirth.

16. "Plague on this bill! I don't believe I have so much cash in the house—Can you give me change for a 100*l.* note?"—"No."—"Then call in as you pass to-morrow."

18. "Not at home."

25. "*Appoint a day!* Pray, what does your master mean? Tell him I'll call upon him, to know what he means by such a message."

April 14. "What! no discount?"—"Sir, it has been due these two years."—"There's your money, then."—"These notes won't pay."—"Then you must call again; I have no loose cash in the house."

And here ends the payment of 9*l.* 14*s.* 6*d.* with three doubtful notes.

But these are only a sample, after all, of the many excuses I must receive; and the most mortifying part of the business is, that such debtors are those who really can pay, but, by various delays, obtain the use of money, and, in some cases, tire out the patience of the creditor. I must say, indeed, that they are remarkably civil: they give me the prettiest words—they send their compliments and kind love "to Mrs. L—— and the dear little ones;" but (plague on them!) they won't send the money.

As my fellow-tradesmen labor under the same hardships, in these respects, as myself, I hope you will not refuse this humble statement of our case; and, if it produces the payment of any one bill, which I should have to hunt after, you will merit the hearty thanks of Mr. Editor,

Your humble servant,
John L****.

Huddersfield, Christmas-day.

FRUITS OF SOLITUDE

IN

REFLECTIONS AND MAXIMS

RELATING TO THE

CONDUCT OF HUMAN LIFE:

BY

WILLIAM PENN

Preface

READER,—

This manual I present thee with is the fruit of solitude, a school few care to learn in, though none instruct us better. Some parts of it are the result of serious reflection; others, the flashings of lucid intervals; written for private satisfaction, and now published for a help to human conduct.

The author blesseth God for his retirement, and kisses that gentle hand that led him into it; for, though it should prove barren to the world, it can never do so to him.

He has now had some time he could call his own, a property he was never so much master of before: in which he has taken a view of himself and the world; and observed wherein he hath hit and missed the mark; what might have been done, what mended, and what avoided, in his human conduct; together with the omissions and excuses of others, as well societies and governments as private families and persons. And he verily thinks, were he to live over his life again, he could not only, with God's grace, serve him, but his neighbor and himself, better than he hath done, and have seven years of his time to spare. And yet, perhaps, he hath not been the worst or the most idle man in the world; nor is he the oldest. And this is the rather said, that it might quicken thee, reader, to lose none of the time that is yet thine.

The author does not pretend to deliver thee an exact piece; his business not being ostentation, but charity. It is miscellaneous in the matter of it, and by no means artificial in the composure. But it contains hints that may serve thee for texts to preach to thyself upon, and which comprehend much of the course of human life: since, whether thou art parent or child, prince or subject, master or servant, single or married, public or private, mean or honorable, rich or poor, prosperous or improsperous, in peace or controversy, in business or solitude; whatever be thy inclination or aversion, practice or duty, thou wilt find something not unsuitably said for thy direction and advantage. Accept and improve what deserves thy notice; the rest excuse, and place to account of good-will to thee and the whole creation of God.

Ignorance

It is admirable to consider how many millions of people come into and go out of the world, ignorant of themselves, and of the world they have lived in.

If one went to see Windsor Castle or Hampton Court, it would be strange not to observe and remember the situation, the building, the gardens, fountains, &c. that make up the beauty and pleasure of such a seat. And yet few people know themselves; no, not their own bodies, the houses of their minds, the most curious structure in the world; a living, walking tabernacle; nor the world of which it was made, and out of which it is fed; which would be so much our benefit, as well as our pleasure, to know. We cannot doubt of this, when we are told that the "invisible things of God are brought to light by the things that are seen;" and, consequently, we read our duty in them, as often as we look upon them, to Him that is the great and wise author of them, if we look as we should do.

The world is certainly a great and stately volume of natural things, and may be not improperly styled the hieroglyphics of a better; but, alas! how very few leaves of it do we seriously turn over! This ought to be the subject of the education of our youth; who, at twenty, when they should be fit for business, know little or nothing of it.

Education*

We are in pain to make them scholars, but not men; to talk, rather than to know; which is true canting.

The first thing obvious to children is what is sensible; and that we make no part of their rudiments.

We press their memory too soon, and puzzle, strain, and load them with words and rules to know grammar and rhetoric, and a strange tongue or two, that it is ten to one may never be useful to them; leaving their natural genius to mechanical, and physical or natural knowledge uncultivated and neglected; which would be of exceeding use and pleasure to them through the whole course of their lives.

To be sure languages are not to be despised or neglected; but, things are still to be preferred.

Children had rather be making tools and instruments of play; shaping, drawing, framing, and building, &c., than getting some rules of propriety of speech by heart; and those also would follow with more judgment, and less trouble and time.

It were happy if we studied nature more in natural things, and acted according to nature, whose rules are few, plain, and most reasonable.

Let us begin where she begins, go her pace, and close always where she ends, and we cannot miss of being good naturalists.

The creation would not be longer a riddle to us. The heavens, earth, and waters, with their respective, various, and numerous inhabitants, their productions, natures, seasons, sympathies, and antipathies, their use, benefit, and pleasure, would be better

---

*Great improvements have been made in books, and in the education of the young and rising generation, since the days of William Penn; and amongst the many who have exercised their ingenuity as well as benevolence in this way, Lindley Murray may be considered as standing pre-eminent; and although some may consider him not to have been so nicely particular in point of science, still, as the main object of this truly benevolent man seems to have been to imbue the young and tender mind with the love of virtue, in this we must acknowledge he has been truly successful, for there is hardly a region or a clime where his juvenile books are not to be found, and by which the present generation has been improved in virtue and piety.

understood by us; and an eternal wisdom, power, majesty, and goodness, very conspicuous to us, through those sensible and passing forms: the world wearing the mark of its Maker, whose stamp is every where visible, and the characters very legible to the children of wisdom.

And it would go a great way to caution and direct people in their use of the world, that they were better studied and known in the creation of it.

For how could men find their confidence to abuse it, while they should see the great Creator stare them in the face, in all and every part thereof?

Their ignorance makes them insensible; and to that insensibility may be ascribed their hard usage of several parts of this noble creation: that has the stamp and voice of a Deity every where, and in every thing, to the observing.

It is pity, therefore, that books have not been composed for youth by some curious and careful naturalists, and also mechanics, in the Latin tongue, to be used in schools, that they might learn things with words; things obvious and familiar to them, and which would make the tongue easier to be obtained by them.

Many able gardeners and husbandmen are ignorant of the reason of their calling, as most artificers are of the reason of their own rules that govern their excellent workmanship. But a naturalist and mechanic of this sort is master of the reason of both; and might be of the practice too, if his industry kept pace with his speculation; which were very commendable, and without which he cannot be said to be a complete naturalist or mechanic.

Finally, if man be the index or epitome of the world, as philosophers tell us, we have only to read ourselves well to be learned in it. But, because there is nothing we less regard than the characters of the Power that made us, which are so clearly written upon us, and the world he has given us, and can best tell us what we are and should be, we are even strangers to our own genius: the glass in which we should see that true, instructing, and agreeable variety, which is to be observed in nature, to the admiration of that wisdom, and adoration of that Power, which made us all.

Pride

And yet we are very apt to be full of ourselves, instead of him that made what we much value; and but for whom we can have no reason to value ourselves. For we have nothing that we can call our own; no, not ourselves; for we are all but tenants, and at will too, of the great Lord of ourselves, and the rest of this great farm, the world that we live upon.

But, methinks, we cannot answer it to ourselves, as well as our Maker, that we should live and die ignorant of ourselves, and thereby of him, and the obligations we are under to him for ourselves.

If the worth of a gift sets the obligation, and directs the return of the party that receives it, he that is ignorant of it will be at a loss to value it, and the giver for it.

Here is a man in his ignorance of himself: he knows not how to estimate his Creator, because he knows not how to value his creation. If we consider his make, and lovely compositure, the several stories of his wonderful structure, his divers members, their order, function, and dependancy; the instruments of food, the vessels of digestion, the several transmutations it passes, and how nourishment is carried and diffused throughout the whole body, by most intricate and imperceptible passages; how the animal spirit is thereby refreshed, and, with an unspeakable dexterity and motion, sets all parts at work to feed themselves; and, last of all, how the rational soul is seated in the animal, as its proper house, as is the animal in the body; I say, if this rare fabric alone were but considered by us, with all the rest by which it is fed and comforted, surely man would have a more reverent sense of the power, wisdom, and goodness of God, and of that duty he owes to him for it. But if he would be acquainted with his own soul, its noble faculties, its union with the body, its nature and end, and the providence by which the whole frame of humanity is preserved, he would admire and adore his good and great God. But man has become a strange contradiction to himself; but it is of himself; not being by constitution, but corruption, such.

He would have others obey him, even his own kind; but he will not obey God, that is so much above him, and who made him.

He will lose none of his authority; no, not abate an ace of it. He is humorsome to his wife, beats his children, is angry with his servants, strict with his neighbors, revenges all affronts to the extremity; but, alas! forgets all the while that he is the man; and is more in arrear to God, that is so very patient with him, than they are to him, with whom he is so strict and impatient.

He is curious to wash, dress, and perfume his body, but careless of his soul; the one shall have many hours, the other not so many minutes; this shall have three or four new suits a year, but that must wear its old clothes still.

If he be to receive or see a great man, how nice and anxious is he that all things be in order; and with what respect and address does he approach and make his court! But to God, how dry and formal, and constrained in his devotion!

In his prayers he says, "Thy will be done;" but means his own: at least acts so.

It is too frequent to begin with God, and end with the world. But he is the good man's beginning and end, he is Alpha and Omega.

Luxury

Such is now become our delicacy, that we will not eat ordinary meat, nor drink small, palled liquor; we must have the best, and the best cooked for our bodies, while our souls feed on empty or corrupted things.

In short, man is spending all upon a bare house, and hath little or no furniture within to recommend it; which is preferring the cabinet to the jewel, a lease of seven years before an inheritance. So absurd a thing is man, after all his proud pretences to wit and understanding.

Inconsideration

The want of due consideration is the cause of all the unhappiness man brings upon himself. For his second thoughts rarely agree with the first; which pass not without a considerable retrenchment or correction. And yet that sensible warning is, too frequently, not precaution enough for his future conduct.

Well may we say, "Our infelicity is of ourselves;" since there is nothing we do that we should not do, but we know it, and yet do it.

Disappointment and Resignation

For disappointments, that come not by our own folly, they are the trials or corrections of Heaven; and it is our own fault if they prove not our advantage.

To repine at them does not mend the matter; it is only to grumble at our Creator. But to see the hand of God in them, with an humble submission to his will, is the way to turn our water to wine, and engage the greatest love and mercy on our side.

We must needs disorder ourselves, if we only look at our losses. But if we consider how little we deserve what is left, our passion will cool, and our murmurs will turn into thankfulness.

If our hairs fall not to the ground, less do we, or our substance, without God's providence.

Nor can we fall below the arms of God, how low soever it be we fall.

For though our Saviour's passion is over, his compassion is not. That never fails his humble, sincere disciples. In him they find more than all that they lose in the world.

Murmuring

Is it reasonable to take it ill that any body desires of us that which is their own? All we have is the Almighty's; and shall not God have his own when he calls for it?

Discontentedness is not only in such a case ingratitude, but injustice; for we are both unthankful for the time we had it, and not honest enough to restore it if we could keep it.

But it is hard for us to look on things in such glass, and at such a distance from this low world and yet it is our duty, and would be our wisdom and our glory, to do so.

Censoriousness

We are apt to be very pert at censuring others, where we will not endure advice ourselves. And nothing shows our weakness more, than to be so sharp-sighted at spying other men's faults, and so purblind about our own.

When the actions of a neighbor are upon the stage, we can have all our wits about us, are so quick and critical we can split a hair, and find out every failure and infirmity; but are without feeling, or have but very little sense, of our own.

Much of this comes from ill-nature, as well as from an inordinate value of ourselves: for we love rambling better than home, and blaming the unhappy rather than covering and relieving them.

In such occasions some show their malice, and are witty upon misfortunes; others their justice, they can reflect apace; but few or none their charity, especially if it be about money matters.

You shall see an old miser come forth with a set gravity, and so much severity against the distressed, to excuse his purse, that he will, ere he has done, put it out of all question that riches is righteousness with him. "This," says he, "is the fruit of your prodigality," (as if, poor man! covetousness were no fault,) "or of your projects, or grasping after a great trade;" while he himself would have done the same thing, but that he had not the courage to venture so much ready money out of his own trusty hands, though it had been to have brought him back the Indies in return. But the proverb is just, "Vice should not correct sin."

They have a right to censure, that have a heart to help: the rest is cruelty, not justice.

Bonds of Charity

Lend not beyond thy ability, nor refuse to lend out of thy ability; especially when it will help others more than it can hurt thee.

If thy debtor be honest and capable, thou hast thy money again, if not with increase, with praise. If he prove insolvent, do not ruin him to get that which it will not ruin thee to lose: for thou art but a steward, and another is thy owner, master, and judge.

The more merciful acts thou dost, the more mercy thou wilt receive; and if, with a charitable employment of thy temporal riches, thou gainest eternal treasure, thy purchase is infinite: thou wilt have found the art of multiplying indeed.

Frugality, or Bounty

Frugality is good, if liberality be joined with it. The first is leaving off superfluous expensés; the last bestowing them to the benefit of others that need. The first without the last begins covetousness; the last without the first begins prodigality. Both together make an excellent temper. Happy the place where that is found.

Were it universal, we should be cured of two extremes—want and excess: and the one would supply the other, and so bring both nearer to a mean; the just degree of earthy happiness.

It is a reproach to religion and government to suffer so much poverty and excess.

Were the superfluities of a nation valued, and made a perpetual tax for benevolence, there would be more alms-houses than poor, schools than scholars, and enough to spare for government besides.

Hospitality is good, if the poorer sort are the subjects of our bounty; else, too near a superfluity.

Discipline

If thou wouldst be happy and easy in thy family, above all things observe discipline.

Every one in it should know their duty, and there should be a time and place for every thing; and, whatever else is done or omitted, be sure to begin and end with God.

Industry

Love labor: for if thou dost not want it for food, thou mayest for physic. It is wholesome for thy body, and good for thy mind. It prevents the fruits of idleness, which many times come of nothing to do, and lead too many to do what is worse than nothing.

A garden, an elaboratory, a workhouse, improvements, and breeding, are pleasant and profitable diversions to the idle and ingenious; for here they miss ill company, and converse with nature and art; whose varieties are equally grateful and instructing, and preserve a good constitution of body and mind.

Temperance

To this a spare diet contributes much. Eat, therefore, to live, and do not live to eat. That is like a man, but this below a beast.

Have wholesome, but not costly food; and be rather cleanly than dainty in ordering it.

The receipts of cookery are swelled to a volume, but a good stomach excels them all: to which nothing contributes more than industry and temperance.

It is a cruel folly to offer up to ostentation so many lives of creatures as make up the state of our treats; as it is a prodigal one to spend more in sauce than in meat.

The proverb says that "Enough is as good as a feast;" but it is certainly better, if superfluity be a fault, which never fails to be at festivals.

If thou rise with an appetite, thou art sure never to sit down without one.

Rarely drink but when thou art dry; nor then, between meals, if it can be avoided.

The smaller the drink, the clearer the head, and the cooler the blood: which are great benefits in temper and business.

Strong liquors are good at some times, and in small proportions: being better for physic than food; for cordials than common use.

The most common things are the most useful; which shows both the wisdom and goodness of the great Lord of the family of the world.

What, therefore, he has made rare, do not use too commonly; lest thou shouldst invert the use and order of things, become wanton and voluptuous, and thy blessings prove a curse.

"Let nothing be lost," said our Saviour; but that is lost that is misused.

Neither urge another to that thou wouldst be unwilling to do thyself; nor do thyself what looks to thee unseemly and intemperate in another.

All excess is ill; but drunkenness is of the worst sort. It spoils health, dismounts the mind, and unmans men. It reveals secrets, is quarrelsome, lascivious, impudent, dangerous, and mad. In fine, he that is drunk is not a man; because he is so long void of reason, that distinguishes a man from a beast.

Apparel

Excess in apparel is another costly folly. The very trimming of the vain world would clothe all the naked one.

Choose thy clothes by thine own eyes, not another's. The more plain and simple they are, the better; neither unshapely, nor fantastical; for use and decency, and not for pride.

If thou art clean and warm, it is sufficient; for more doth but rob the poor, and pleases the wanton.

It is said of the true church, "The King's daughter is all glorious within." Let our care, therefore, be of our minds, more than
of our bodies, if we would be of her communion.

We are told, with truth, that "Meekness and modesty are the
rich and charming attire of the soul;" and the plainer the dress,
the more distinctly, and with greater lustre, their beauty shines.

It is great pity such beauties are so rare, and those of Jezebel's
forehead are so common; whose dresses are incentives to lust;
but bars, instead of motives, to love or virtue.

Right Marriage

Never marry but for love; but see that thou lovest what is lovely.

If love be not thy chiefest motive, thou wilt soon grow weary
of a married state, and stray from thy promise, to search out thy
pleasures in forbidden places.

Let not enjoyment lessen, but augment, affection: it being the
basest of passions to like when we have not, what we slight when
we possess.

It is the difference betwixt lust and love: this is fixed, that
volatile. Love grows, lust wastes, by enjoyment; and the reason
is, that one springs from an union of souls, and the other springs
from an union of sense.

They have divers originals, and so are of different families:
that, inward and deep; this, superficial: this, transient; and that,
permanent.

They that marry for money cannot have the true satisfaction
of marriage; the requisite means being wanting.

Men are generally more careful of the breed of their horses
and dogs than of their children.

Those must be of the best sort, for shape, strength, courage,
and good conditions; but as for these, their own posterity,
money shall answer all things. With such, it makes the crooked
straight, sets squint eyes right, cures madness, covers folly,
changes ill conditions, mends the skin, gives a sweet breath,
repairs honor, makes young, works wonders.

O, how sordid is man grown! man, the noblest creature of the world, as a God on earth, and the image of him that made it, thus to mistake earth for heaven, and worship gold for God.

Avarice

Covetousness is the greatest of monsters, as well as the root of all evil. I have once seen the man who died to save charges! "What! give ten shillings to a doctor, and have an apothecary's bill besides, that may come to I know not what!" No, not he: valuing life less than twenty shillings. But, indeed, such a man could not well set too low a price upon himself; who, though he lived up to the chin in bags, had rather die than find in his heart to open one of them, to help to save his life.

Such a man is "felo de se," and deserves not Christian burial.

He is a common nuisance; a way across the stream, that stops the current; an obstruction, to be removed by a purge of the law. The only gratification he gives his neighbors, is to let them see that he himself is as little the better for what he has as they are; for he always looks like Lent, a sort of Lay-Minim. In some sense, he may be compared to Pharaoh's lean kine; for all that he has does him no good. He commonly wears his clothes till they leave him, or that nobody else can wear them. He affects to be thought poor, to escape robbery and taxes; and by looking as if he wanted an alms, to excuse himself from giving any. He ever goes late to markets, to cover buying the worst; but does it because that is cheapest. He lives on the offal. His life were an insupportable punishment to any temper but his own; and no greater torment to him on earth, than to live as other men do. But the misery of his pleasure is, that he is never satisfied with getting, and always in fear of losing what he cannot use.

How vilely he has lost himself, that becomes a slave to his servant, and exalts him to the dignity of his Maker! Gold is the god, the wife, the friend of the money-monger of the world. But in [. . .]

[. . .] Marriage,

Do thou be wise. Prefer the person before money, virtue before beauty, the mind before the body: then thou hast a wife, a friend, a companion, a second self, one that bears an equal share with thee in all thy toils and troubles.

Choose one that measures her satisfaction, safety, and danger, by thine; and of whom thou art sure, as of thy most secret thoughts: a friend as well as a wife: which, indeed, a wife implies; for she is but half a wife that is not, or is not capable of being, such a friend.

Sexes make no difference; since in souls there is none: and they are the subjects of friendship.

He that minds a body, and not a soul, has not the better part of that relation; and will consequently want the noblest comfort of a married life.

The satisfaction of our senses is low, short, and transient: but the mind gives a more raised and extended pleasure, and is capable of a happiness founded upon reason, not bounded and limited by the circumstances that bodies are confined to.

Here it is we ought to search out our pleasure, where the field is large and full of variety, and of an enduring nature: sickness, poverty, or disgrace being not able to shake it, because it is not under the moving influences of worldly contingencies.

The satisfaction of those that do so is in well-doing, and in the assurance they have of a future reward; that they are best loved by those they love most; and that they enjoy and value the liberty of their minds above that of their bodies: having the whole creation for their prospect; the most noble and wonderful works and providences of God, the histories of the ancients, and in them the actions, and examples of the virtuous; and, lastly, themselves, their affairs and family, to exercise their minds and friendship upon.

Nothing can be more entire and without reserve; nothing more zealous, affectionate, and sincere; nothing more contented and constant, than such a couple; nor no greater temporal felicity than to be one of them.

Between a man and his wife, nothing ought to rule but
love. Authority is for children and servants; yet not without
sweetness.

As love ought to bring them together, so it is the best way to
keep them well together.

Wherefore, use her not as a servant, whom thou wouldst, perhaps, have served seven years to have obtained.

A husband and wife that love and value one another show
their children and servants that they should do so too. Others
visibly lose their authority in their families by their contempt of
one another, and teach their children to be unnatural by their
own examples.

It is a general fault, not to be more careful to preserve nature
in children; who, at least in the second descent, hardly have a
feeling of their relation; which must be an unpleasant reflection
to affectionate parents.

Frequent visits, presents, intimate correspondence, and
intermarriages within allowed bounds, are means of keeping up
the concern and affection that nature requires from relations.

Friendship

Friendship is the next pleasure we may hope for; and where we
find it not at home, or have no home to find it in, we may seek
it abroad. It is an union of spirits, a marriage of hearts, and the
bond thereof virtue.

There can be no friendship where there is no freedom.
Friendship loves a free air, and will not be penned up in strait
and narrow enclosures. It will speak freely, and act so too; and
take nothing ill where no ill is meant; nay, where it is, it will easily forgive, and forget too, upon small acknowledgments.

Friends are true twins in soul; they sympathize in every thing,
and have the same love and aversion.

One is not happy without the other; nor can either of them be
miserable alone. As if they could change bodies, they take their
turns in pain as well as in pleasure; relieving one another in their
most adverse conditions.

What one enjoys, the other cannot want. Like the primitive Christians, they have all things in common, and no property but in one another.

Qualities of a Friend

A true friend unbosoms freely, advises justly, assists readily, adventures boldly, takes all patiently, defends courageously, and continues a friend unchangeably.

These being the qualities of a friend, we are to find them before we choose one.

The covetous, the angry, the proud, the jealous, the talkative, cannot but make ill friends, as well as false.

In short, choose a friend as thou dost a wife, till death separate you.

Yet be not a friend beyond the altar, but let virtue bound thy friendship; else it is not friendship, but an evil confederacy.

If my brother or kinsman will be my friend, I ought to prefer him before a stranger; or I show little duty or nature to my parents.

And as we ought to prefer our kindred in point of affection, so too in point of charity, if equally needing and deserving.

Caution and Conduct

Be not easily acquainted; lest, finding reason to cool, thou makest an enemy instead of a good neighbor.

Be reserved, but not sour; grave, but not formal; bold, but not rash; humble, but not servile; patient, not insensible; constant, not obstinate; cheerful, not light; rather sweet than familiar; familiar than intimate; and intimate with very few, and upon very good grounds.

Return the civilities thou receivest, and be ever grateful for favors.

Reparation

If thou hast done an injury to another, rather own it than defend it. One way thou gainest forgiveness; the other, thou doublest the wrong and reckoning.

Some oppose honor to submission, but it can be no honor to maintain what it is dishonorable to do.

To confess a fault that is none, out of fear, is indeed mean; but not to be afraid of standing in one, is brutish.

We should make more haste to right our neighbor, than we do to wrong him; and instead of being vindictive, we should leave him to judge of his own satisfaction.

True honor will pay treble damages rather than justify one wrong by another.

In such controversies, it is but too common for some to say "Both are to blame," to excuse their own unconcernedness; which is a base neutrality. Others will cry, "They are both alike;" thereby involving the injured with the guilty, to mince the matter for the faulty, or cover their own injustice to the wronged party.

Fear and gain are great perverters of mankind; and where either prevails, the judgment is violated.

Rules of Conversation

Avoid company, where it is not profitable or necessary; and, on those occasions, speak little, and last.

Silence is wisdom where speaking is folly, and always safe.

Some are so foolish as to interrupt and anticipate those that speak, instead of hearing and thinking before they answer, which is uncivil as well as silly.

If thou thinkest twice before thou speakest once, thou wilt speak twice the better for it.

Better say nothing than not to the purpose; and to speak pertinently, consider both what is fit, and when it is fit, to speak.

In all debates, let truth be thy aim; not victory, or an unjust interest: and endeavor to gain, rather than to expose, thy antagonist.

Give no advantage in argument, nor lose any that is offered. This is a benefit which arises from temper.

Do not use thyself to dispute against thine own judgment, to show wit; lest it prepare thee to be too indifferent about what is right: nor against another man, to vex him, or for mere trial of skill; since to inform, or to be informed, ought to be the end of all conferences.

Men are too apt to be more concerned for their credit than for the cause.

Eloquence

There is a truth and beauty in rhetoric; but it oftener serves ill turns than good ones.

Elegancy is a good mien and address given to matter, be it by proper or by figurative speech: where the words are apt, and allusions very natural, certainly it has a moving grace; but it is too artificial for simplicity, and oftentimes for truth. The danger is, lest it delude the weak; who, in such cases, may mistake the handmaid for the mistress, if not error for truth.

It is certain, truth is least indebted to it, because she has least need of it, and least uses it.

But it is a reprovable delicacy in them that despise truth in plain clothes.

Such luxuriants have but false appetites; like those gluttons that, by sauce, force them where they have no stomach, and sacrifice to their palate, not their health: which cannot be without great vanity, nor that without some sin.

Temper

Nothing does reason more right than the coolness of those that offer it; for truth often suffers more by the heat of its defenders, than from the arguments of its opposers.

Zeal ever follows an appearance of truth, and the assured are too apt to be warm: but it is their weak side in argument; zeal being better shown against sin than persons, or their mistakes.

Truth

Where thou art obliged to speak, be sure to speak the truth; for equivocation is half way to lying, as lying is the whole way to hell.

Justice

Believe nothing against another, but upon good authority; nor report what may hurt another, unless it be a greater hurt to others to conceal it.

Secrecy

It is wise not to seek a secret, and honest not to reveal one.
Only trust thyself, and another shall not betray thee.
Openness has the mischief, though not the malice of treachery.

Complacency

Never assent merely to please others; for that is, besides flattery, oftentimes untruth, and discovers a mind to be servile and base: nor contradict to vex others; for that shows an ill temper, and provokes, but profits nobody.

Shifts

Do not accuse others, to excuse thyself; for that is neither generous nor just. But let sincerity and ingenuousness be thy refuge, rather than craft and falsehood; for cunning borders very near upon knavery.

Wisdom never uses nor wants it. Cunning to the wise is as an ape to the man.

Interest

Interest has the security, though not the virtue, of a principal. As the world goes, it is the surest side; for men daily leave both relations and religion to follow it.

It is an odd sight, but very evident, that families and nations of cross religions and humors unite against those of their own, where they find an interest to do it.

We are tied down by our senses to this world; and where that is in question, it can be none with worldly men, whether they should not forsake all other considerations for it.

Inquiry

Have a care of vulgar errors. Dislike, as well as allow, reasonably.

Inquiry is human, blind obedience brutal. Truth never loses by the one, but often suffers by the other.

The most useful truths are plainest; and while we keep to them, our differences cannot rise high.

There may be a wantonness in search, as well as stupidity in trusting. It is great wisdom equally to avoid the extremes.

Right Timing

Do nothing improperly. Some are witty, kind, cold, angry, easy, stiff, jealous, careless, cautious, confident, close, open, but all in the wrong place.

It is ill mistaking, where the matter is of importance.

It is not enough that a thing be right, if it be not fit to be done. If not prudent, though just, it is not advisable. He that loses by getting, had better lose than get.

Knowledge

Knowledge is the treasure, but judgment the treasurer, of a wise man.

He that has more knowledge than judgment, is made for another man's use more than his own.

It cannot be a good constitution, where the appetite is great and the digestion weak.

There are some men like dictionaries, to be looked into upon occasions; but have no connexion, and are little entertaining.

Less knowledge than judgment will always have the advantage upon the injudicious, knowing man.

A wise man makes what he learns his own; the other shows he is but a copy, or a collection at most.

Wit

Wit is a happy and striking way of expressing a thought.

It is not often, though it be lively and mantling, that it carries a great body with it.

Wit, therefore, is fitter for diversion than business, being more grateful to fancy than judgment.

Less judgment than wit, is more sail than ballast.

Yet it must be confessed that wit gives an edge to sense, and recommends it extremely.

Where judgment has wit to express it, there is the best orator.

Obedience to Parents

If thou wouldst be obeyed, being a father; being a son, be obedient.

He that begets thee, owns thee, and has a natural right over thee.

Next to God, thy parents; next to them, the magistrate.

Remember that thou art not more indebted to thy parents for thy nature, than for their love and care.

Rebellion, therefore, in children, was made death by God's law; and in the people, the next thing to idolatry, which is renouncing God, the great parent of all.

Obedience to parents is not only our duty, but our interest. If we received our life from them, we prolong it by obeying them; for obedience is the first commandment with promise.

The obligation is as indissoluble as the relation.

If we must not disobey God to obey them, at least we must let them see that there is nothing else in our refusal; for some unjust commands cannot excuse the general neglect of our duty. They will be our parents, and we must be their children still; and if we cannot act for them against God, neither can we act against them for ourselves, or any thing else.

Bearing

A man in business must put up with many affronts, if he loves his own quiet.

We must not pretend to see all that we see, if we would be easy.

It were endless to dispute upon every thing that is disputable.

A vindictive temper is not only uneasy to others, but to them that have it.

Promising

Rarely promise; but, if lawful, constantly perform.

Hasty resolutions are of the nature of vows; and to be equally avoided.

"I will never do this," says one, yet does it. "I am resolved to do that," says another; but flags upon second thoughts; or does it, though awkwardly, for his word's sake; as if it were worse to break his word, than to do amiss in keeping it.

Wear none of thine own chains; but keep free, whilst thou art free.

It is an effect of passion that wisdom corrects, to lay thyself under resolutions that cannot be well made, and worse performed.

Fidelity

Avoid, all thou canst, being intrusted; but do thy utmost to discharge the trust thou undertakest; for carelessness is injurious, if not unjust.

The glory of a servant is fidelity, which cannot be without diligence, as well as truth.

Fidelity has enfranchised slaves, and adopted servants to be sons.

Reward a good servant well; and rather quit than disquiet thyself with an ill one.

Master

Mix kindness with authority; and rule more by discretion than rigor.

If thy servant be faulty, strive rather to convince him of his error, than to discover thy passion; and when he is sensible, forgive him.

Remember he is thy fellow-creature; and that God's goodness, not thy merit, has made the difference betwixt thee and him.

Let not thy children domineer over thy servants; nor suffer them to slight thy children.

Suppress tales in the general; but where a matter requires notice, encourage the complaint, and right the aggrieved.

If a child, he ought to entreat, not to command; if a servant, to comply, where he does not obey.

Though there should be but one master and mistress in a family, yet servants should know that children have the reversion.

Servant

Indulge not unseemly things in thy master's children, nor refuse them what is fitting; for one is the highest unfaithfulness, and the other indiscretion, as well as disrespect.

Do thine own work honestly and cheerfully; and when that is done, help thy fellow, that so another time he may help thee.

If thou wilt be a good servant, thou must be true; and thou canst not be true, if thou defraudest thy master.

A master may be defrauded many ways by a servant; as in time, care, pains, money, trust.

But a trust servant is the contrary; he is diligent, careful, trusty. He tells no tales, reveals no secrets, refuses no pains, is not to be tempted by gain, or awed by fear, to unfaithfulness.

Such a servant serves God, in serving his master; and has double wages for his work: to wit, here and hereafter.

Jealousy

Be not faincifully jealous, for that is foolish; as to be reasonably so, is wise.

He that superfines upon other men's actions, cozens himself, as well as injures them.

To be very subtle and scrupulous in business, is as hurtful as being over-confident and secure.

In difficult cases, such a temper is timorous; and in despatch, irresolute.

Experience is a safe guide; and a practical head is a great happiness in business.

Posterity

We are too careless of posterity; not considering that as they are, so the next generation will be.

If we would amend the world, we should mend ourselves; and teach our children to be, not what we are, but what they should be.

We are too apt to awaken and tune up their passions by the example of our own; and to teach them to be pleased, not with what is best, but with what pleases best.

It is our duty, and ought to be our care, to ward against that passion in them which is more especially our own weakness and affliction; for we are in great measure accountable for them, as well as for ourselves.

We are in this, also, true turners of the world upside down; for money is first, and virtue last, and least in our care.

It is not how we leave our children, but what we leave them.

To be sure, virtue is but a supplement, and not a principal, in their portion and character; and therefore we see little wisdom or goodness among the rich, in proportion to their wealth.

A Country Life

The country life is to be preferred, for there we see the works of God; but in cities, little else but the works of men; and the one makes a better subject for our contemplation than the other.

As puppets are to men, and babies to children, so is man's workmanship to God's; we are the picture, he the reality.

God's works declare his power, wisdom, and goodness; but man's works, for the most part, his pride, folly, and excess. The one is for use; the other, chiefly, for ostentation and lust.

The country is both the philosopher's garden and library, in which he reads and contemplates the power, wisdom, and goodness of God.

It is his food, as well as study; and gives him life, as well as learning.

A sweet and natural retreat from noise and talk, and allows opportunity for reflection, and gives the best subjects for it.

In short, it is an original, and the knowledge and improvement of it man's oldest business and trade, and the best he can be of.

Art and Project

Art is good, where it is beneficial. Socrates wisely bounded his knowledge and instruction by practice.

Have a care, therefore, of projects; and yet despise nothing rashly, or in the lump.

Ingenuity, as well as religion, sometimes suffers between two thieves: pretenders and despisers.

Though injudicious and dishonest projectors often discredit art, yet the most useful and extraordinary inventions have not at least escaped the scorn of ignorance; as their authors rarely have cracking of their heads, or breaking of their backs.

Undertake no experiment in speculation that appears not true in art; nor then at thine own cost, if costly or hazardous in making.

As many hands make light work, so several purses make cheap experiments.

Industry

Industry is certainly very commendable, and supplies the want of parts.

Patience and diligence, like faith, remove mountains.

Never give out while there is hope; but hope not beyond reason, for that shows more desire than judgment.

It is profitable wisdom to know when we have done enough: much time and pains are spared in not flattering ourselves against probabilities.

Temporal Happiness

Do good with what thou hast, or it will do thee no good.

Seek not to be rich, but happy. The one lies in bags; the other in content, which wealth can never give.

We are apt to call things by wrong names. We will have prosperity to be happiness, and adversity to be misery; though that is the school of wisdom, and oftentimes the way to eternal happiness.

If thou wouldst be happy, bring thy mind to thy condition, and have an indifference for more than what is sufficient.

Have but little to do, and do it thyself; and do to others as thou wouldst have them do to thee: so thou canst not fail of temporal felicity.

The generality are the worse for their plenty. The voluptuous consumes it, the miser hides it: it is the good man that uses it, and to good purposes. But such are hardly found among the prosperous.

Be rather bountiful than expensive.

Neither make nor go to feasts; but let the laborious poor bless thee at home in their solitary cottages.

Never voluntarily want what thou hast in possession; nor so spend it as to involve thyself in want unavoidable.

Be not tempted to presume by success; for many, that have got largely, have lost all by coveting to get more.

To hazard much to get much, has more of avarice than wisdom.

It is great prudence both to bound and use prosperity.

Too few know when they have enough; and fewer know how to employ it.

It is equally advisable not to part lightly with what is hardly gotten, and not to shut up closely what flows in freely.

Act not the shark upon thy neighbor, nor take advantage of the ignorance, prodigality, or necessity of any one; for that is next door to a fraud, and, at best, makes but an unblessed gain.

It is oftentimes the judgment of God upon greedy rich men,

that he suffers them to push on their desires of wealth to the excess of overreaching, grinding, or oppression; which poisons all they have gotten: so that it commonly runs away as fast, and by as bad ways, as it was heaped up together.

Respect

Never esteem any man, or thyself, the more for money; nor think the meaner of thyself, or another, for want of it: virtue being the just reason of respecting, and the want of it of slighting, any one.

A man, like a watch, is to be valued for his goings.

He that prefers him upon other accounts bows to an idol.

Unless virtue guide us, our choice must be wrong.

An able bad man is an ill instrument, and to be shunned as the plague.

Be not deceived with the first appearance of things; but give thyself time to be in the right.

Show is not substance: realities govern wise men.

Have a care, therefore, where there is more sail than ballast.

Hazard

In all business, it is best to put nothing to hazard: but where it is unavoidable, be not rash, by firm and resigned.

We should not be troubled for what we cannot help; but if it was our fault, let it be so no more.

Amendment is repentance, if not reparation.

As a desperate game needs an able gamester, so consideration often would prevent what the best skill in the world cannot recover.

Where the probability of advantage exceeds not that of loss, wisdom never adventures.

To shoot well flying, is well; but to choose it, has more of vanity than judgment.

To be dexterous in danger, is a virtue; but to court danger to show it, is weakness.

Detraction

Have a care of that base evil, detraction. It is the fruit of envy, as that is of pride, the immediate offspring of the Devil; who, of an angel, a Lucifer, a son of the morning, made himself a serpent, a Devil, a Beelzebub, and all that is noxious to the eternal Goodness.

Virtue is not secure against envy. Men will lessen what they will not imitate.

Dislike what deserves it; but never hate, for that is of the nature of malice, which is almost ever to persons, not things; and is one of the blackest qualities sin begets in the soul.

Moderation

It were a happy day if men could bound and qualify their resentments with charity to the offender: for then our anger would be without sin, and better convict and edify the guilty; which alone can make it lawful.

Not to be provoked, is best; but if moved, never correct till the fume is spent; for every stroke our fury strikes is sure to hit ourselves at last.

If we did but observe the allowances our reason makes upon reflection, when our passion is over, we could not want a rule how to behave ourselves again on the like occasion.

We are more prone to complain than redress, and to censure than excuse.

It is next to unpardonable, that we can so often blame what

we will not once mend. It shows that we know, but will not do, our Master's will.

They that censure, should practise; or else, let them heave the first stone, and the last too.

Trick

Nothing needs a trick, but a trick; sincerity loathes one.

We must take care to do things rightly; for a just sentence may be unjustly executed.

Circumstances give great light to true judgment, if well weighed.

Passion

Passion is a sort of fever in the mind, which ever leaves us weaker than it found us.

But, being intermitting, to be sure it is curable with care.

It, more than any thing, deprives us of the use of our judgment: for it raises a dust very hard to see through.

Like wine, whose lees fly up, being jogged, it is too muddy to drink.

It may not unfitly be termed the mob of the man, that commits a riot upon his reason.

I have oftentimes thought that a passionate man is like a weak spring that cannot stand long locked.

And it is as true, that those things are unfit for use, that cannot bear small knocks without breaking.

He that will not hear, cannot judge; and he that cannot bear contradiction, may, with all his wit, miss the mark.

Objection and debate sift our truth; which needs temper as well as judgment.

But, above all, observe it in resentments; for there passion is most extravagant.

Never chide for anger, but instruction.

He that corrects out of passion, raises revenge sooner than repentance.

It has more of wantonness than wisdom; and resembles those that eat to please their palate rather than their appetite.

It is the difference between a wise and a weak man; this judges by the lump, that by parts and their connexion.

The Greeks used to say, "All cases are governed by their circumstances." The same thing may be well and ill, as they change vary the matter.

A man's strength is shown by his bearing,—"Bonum agere, et mala pati, regis est."

Personal Cautions

Reflect without malice, but never without need.

Despise nobody, nor any condition; lest it come to be thy own.

Never rail nor taunt: the one is rude, the other is scornful, and both evil.

Be not provoked by injuries to commit them.

Upbraid only ingratitude.

Haste makes work, which caution prevents.

Tempt no man, lest thou fall for it.

Have a care of presuming upon after-games; for if that miss, all is gone. Opportunities should never be lost, because they can hardly be gained.

It is well to cure, but better to prevent a distemper. The first shows more skill, but the last more wisdom.

Never make a trial of skill in difficult or hazardous cases.

Refuse not to be informed, for that shows pride or stupidity.

Humility and knowledge in poor clothes excel pride and ignorance in costly attire.

Neither despise nor oppose what thou dost not understand.

Balance

We must not be concerned above the value of the thing that engages us; nor raised above reason, in maintaining what we think reasonable.

It is too common an error, to invert the order of things, by making an end of that which is a means, and a means of that which is an end.

Religion and government escape not this mischief; the first is too often made a means instead of an end; the other an end, instead of a means.

Thus men seek wealth rather than subsistence; and the end of clothes is the least reason of their use. Nor is the satisfying of our appetite our end in eating, so much as the pleasing of our palate. The like may be also said of building, furniture, &c., where the man rules not the beast, and appetite submits not to reason.

It is great wisdom to proportion our esteem to the nature of the thing; for, as that way things will not be undervalued, so neither will they engage us above their intrinsic worth.

If we suffer little things to have great hold upon us, we shall be as much transported for them as if they deserved it.

It is an old proverb, "Maxima bella ex lavissimis causis;"—the greatest feuds have had the smallest beginnings.

No matter what the subject of the dispute be, but what place we give it in our minds; for that governs our concern and resentment.

It is one of the most fatal errors of our lives, when we spoil a good cause by an ill management; and it is not impossible but we may mean well in an ill business, but that will not defend it.

If we are but sure the end is right, we are too apt to gallop over all bounds to compass it; not considering that lawful ends may be very unlawfully attained.

Let us be careful to take just ways to compass just things, that they may last in their benefits to us.

There is a troublesome humor some men have, that if they

may not lead they will not follow; but had rather a thing were never done, than not done their own way, though otherwise very desirable.

This comes of an over-fulness of ourselves, and shows we are more concerned for praise than the success of what we think a good thing.

Popularity

Affect not to be seen, and men will less see thy weakness.

They that show more than they are, raise an expectation they cannot answer; and so lose their credit as soon as they are found out.

Avoid popularity: it has many snares, and no real benefit to thyself, and uncertainty to others.

Privacy

Remember the proverb, "Bene qui latuit, bene vixit;"—they are happy that live retiredly.

If this be true, princes and their grandees, of all men, are the unhappiest, for they live least alone: and they that must be enjoyed by every body can never enjoy themselves as they should.

It is the advantage little men have upon them; they can be private, and have leisure for family comforts, which are the greatest worldly contents men can enjoy.

But they that place pleasure in greatness seek it there; and we see, rule is as much the ambition of some natures, as privacy is the choice of others.

Government

Government has many shapes; but it is sovereignty, though not freedom, in all of them.

Rex and Tyrannus are very different characters: one rules his people by laws, to which they consent; the other by his absolute will and power. That is called freedom; this, tyranny.

The first is endangered by the ambition of the populace, which shakes the constitution; the other by an ill administration, which hazards the tyrant and his family.

It is great wisdom, in princes of both sorts, not to strain points too high with their people; for whether the people have a right to oppose them or not, they are ever sure to attempt it when things are carried too far; though the remedy oftentimes proves worse than the disease.

Happy that king who is great by justice, and the people who are free by obedience.

Where the ruler is just, he may be strict; else it is two to one it turns upon him: and though he should prevail, he can be no gainer where his people are the losers.

Where example keeps pace with authority, power hardly fails to be obeyed, and magistrates to be honored.

Princes must not have passions in government, nor resent beyond interest and religion.

Let the people think they govern, and they will be governed.

This cannot fail, if those they trust are trusted.

That prince who is just to them in great things, and humors them oftentimes in small ones, is sure to have and keep them from all the world.

For the people are the politic wife of the prince, that may be better managed by wisdom than ruled by force.

But where the magistrate is partial, and serves ill turns, he loses his authority with the people, and gives the populace opportunity to gratify their ambition; and so lays a stumbling-block for his people to fall.

It is true, that where a subject is more popular than the prince, the prince is in danger; but it is as true, that it is his own fault; for nobody has the like means, interest, or reason, to be as popular as he.

It is an unaccountable thing, that some princes incline rather to be feared than loved; when they see that fear does not oftener secure a prince against the dissatisfaction of his people, than love makes a subject too many for such a prince.

Certainly, service upon inclination is like to go farther than obedience upon compulsion.

The Romans had a just sense of this, when they placed Optimus before Maximus, to their most illustrious captains and Cæsars.

Besides, experience tells us that goodness raises a nobler passion in the soul, and gives a better sense of duty, than severity.

What did Pharaoh get, by increasing the Israelites' task? Ruin to himself in the end.

Kings, chiefly in this, should imitate God: their mercy should be above all their works.

The difference between the prince and the peasant is in this world; but a temper ought to be observed by him that has the advantage here, because of the judgment of the next.

The end of every thing should direct the means; now, that of government being the good of the whole, nothing less should be the aim of the prince.

As often as rulers endeavor to attain just ends by just mediums, they are sure of a quiet and easy government; and as sure of convulsions, where the nature of things are violated, and the order overruled.

It is certain, princes ought to have great allowances made them for faults in government, since they see by other people's eyes, and hear by their ears; but ministers of state, their immediate confidants and instruments, have much to answer for, if, to gratify private passions, they misguide the prince to do public injury.

Ministers of state should undertake their posts at their peril. If princes overrule them, let them show the law, and humbly resign; if fear, gain, or flattery prevail, let them answer it to the law.

The prince cannot be preserved, but where the minister is punishable; for people as well as princes will not endure "imperium in imperio."

If ministers are weak or ill men, and so spoil their places, it is the prince's fault that chose them; but if their places spoil them, it is their own fault to be made worse by them.

It is but just, that those that reign by their princes should suffer for their princes; for it is a safe and necessary maxim, not to shift heads in government, while the hands are in being that should answer for them.

And yet it were intolerable to be a minister of state, if every body may be accuser and judge.

Let, therefore, the false accuser no more escape an exemplary punishment than the guilty minister.

For it profanes government to have the credit of the leading men in it subject to vulgar censure, which is often ill-grounded.

The safety of a prince, therefore, consists in a well-chosen council; and that only can be said to be so, where the persons that compose it are qualified for the business that comes before them.

Who would send to a tailor to make a lock, or to a smith to make a suit of clothes?

Let there be merchants for trade, seamen for the admiralty, travellers for foreign affairs, some of the leading men of the country for home business, and common and civil lawyers to advise of legality and right, who should always keep to the strict rules of law.

Three things contribute much to ruin government: looseness, oppression, and envy.

Where the reins of government are too slack, there the manners of the people are corrupted; and that destroys industry, begets effeminacy, and provokes Heaven against it.

Oppression makes a poor country and desperate people, who always wait an opportunity to change.

"He that ruleth over men must be just, ruling in the fear of God," said an old and wise king.

Envy disturbs and distracts government, clogs the wheels, and perplexes the administration; and nothing contributes more to this disorder than a partial distribution of rewards and punishments in the sovereign.

As it is not reasonable that men should be compelled to serve, so those that have employments should not be endured to leave them humorsomely.

Where the state intends a man no affront, he should not affront the state.

A Private Life

A private life is to be preferred; the honor and gain of public posts bearing no proportion with the comfort of it. The one is free and quiet, the other servile and noisy.

It was a great answer of the Shunamite woman, "I dwell among my own people."

They that live of their own, neither need, nor often list, to wear the livery of the public.

Their subsistence is not during pleasure, nor have they patrons to please or present.

If they are not advanced, neither can they be disgraced; and as they know not the smiles of majesty, so they feel not the frowns of greatness, nor the effects of envy.

If they want the pleasures of a court, they also escape the temptations of it.

Private men, in fine, are so much their own, that, paying common dues, they are sovereigns of all the rest.

A Public Life

Yet the public must and will be served; and they that do it well deserve public marks of honor and profit. To do so, men must have public minds as well as salaries; or they will serve private ends at public cost.

Government can never be well administered, but where those intrusted make conscience of well discharging their places.

Qualifications

Five things are requisite to a good officer: ability, clean hands, despatch, patience, and impartiality.

Capacity

He that understands not his employment, whatever else he knows, must be unfit for it; and the public suffer by his inexpertness.

They that are able should be just too; or the government may be the worse for their capacity.

Clean Hands

Covetousness in such men prompts them to prostitute the public for gain.

The taking of a bribe, or gratuity, should be punished with as severe penalties as the defrauding of the state.

Let men have sufficient salaries, and exceed them at their peril.

It is a dishonor to government, that its officers should live on benevolence; as it ought to be infamous for officers to dishonor the public, by being twice paid for the same business.

But to be paid and not do business, is rank oppression.

Despatch

Despatch is a great and good quality in an officer, where duty, not gain, excites it. But of this too many make their private market, and overplus to their wages. Thus the salary is for doing, and the bribe for despatching, the business; as if business could be done before it was despatched; or they were to be paid apart, one by the government, the other by the party.

Despatch is as much the duty of an officer as doing, and very much the honor of the government he serves.

Delays have been more injurious than direct injustice.

They too often starve those they dare not deny.

The very winner is made a loser, because he pays twice for his own; like those that purchase estates mortgaged before to the full value.

Our law says well, "To delay justice, is injustice."

Not to have a right, and not to come at it, differ little.

Refusal, or despatch, is the duty and wisdom of a good officer.

Patience

Patience is a virtue every where; but it shines with greatest lustre in the men of government.

Some are so proud or testy, they will not hear what they should redress.

Others are so weak, they sink or burst under the weight of their office; though they can lightly run away with the salary of it.

Business can never be well done that is not well understood; which cannot be without patience.

It is cruelty, indeed, not to give the unhappy a hearing, when we ought to help; but it is the top of oppression to browbeat the humble and modest miserable, when they seek relief.

Some, it is true, are unreasonable in their desires and hopes; but then we should inform, not rail at and reject them.

It is, therefore, as great an instance of wisdom as a man in business can give, to be patient under the impertinences and contradictions that attend it.

Method goes far to prevent trouble in business; for it makes the task easy, hinders confusion, saves abundance of time, and instructs those that have business depending what to do and what to hope.

Impartiality

Impartiality, though it be the last, is not the least part of the character of a good magistrate.

It is noted as a fault in Holy Writ, even to regard the poor in judgment: how much more the rich?

If our compassion must not sway us, less should our fears, profits, or prejudices.

Justice is justly represented blind, because she sees no difference in the parties concerned.

She has but one scale and weight for rich and poor, great and small.

Her sentence is not guided by the person, but the cause.

The impartial judge, in judgment, knows nothing but the law; the prince, no more than the peasant; his kindred, than a stranger. Nay, his enemy is sure to be on equal terms with his friend, when he is upon the bench.

Impartiality is the life of justice, as that is of government.

Nor is it only a benefit to the state; for private families cannot subsist comfortably without it.

Parents that are partial are ill obeyed by their children; and partial masters not better served by their servants.

Partiality is always indirect, if not dishonest; for it shows a bias, where reason would have none; if not an injury, which justice every where forbids.

As it makes favorites without reason, so it uses no reason in judging of actions: confirming the proverb, "The crow thinks her own bird the fairest."

What some see to be no fault in one, they will have criminal in another.

Nay, how ugly do our failings look to us in the persons of others, which yet we see not in ourselves.

And but too common it is for some people not to know their own maxims and principles in the mouths of other men, when they give occasion to use them.

Partiality corrupts our judgment of persons and things, of ourselves and others.

It contributes more than any thing to factions in the government and feuds in families.

It is a prodigal passion, that seldom returns till it is hunger-bit, and disappointments bring it within bounds.

And yet we may be indifferent to a fault.

Indifference

Indifference is good in judgment, but bad in relation, and stark naught in religion.

And even in judgment, our indifference must be to the persons, not causes; for one, to be sure, is right.

Neutrality

Neutrality is something else than indifference; and yet of kin to it too.

A judge ought to be indifferent, and yet he cannot be said to be neutral.

The one being to be even in judgment; and the other, not to meddle at all. And where it is lawful, to be sure, it is best to be neutral.

He that espouses parties, can hardly divorce himself from their fate; and more fall with their party than rise with it.

A wise neuter joins with neither, but uses both, as his honest interest leads him.

A neuter only has room to be a peace-maker, for, being of neither side, he has the means of mediating a reconciliation of both.

A Party

And yet, where right or religion gives a call, a neuter must be a coward or a hypocrite.

In such cases, we should never be backward, nor yet mistaken.

When our right or religion is in question, then is the fittest time to assert it.

Nor must we always be neutral where our neighbor is concerned; for though meddling is a fault, helping is a duty.

We have a call to do good, as often as we have the power and occasion.

If Heathens could say, "We are not born for ourselves," surely Christians should practise it.

They are taught so by his example as well as doctrine, from whom they have borrowed their name.

Ostentation

Do what good thou canst unknown, and be not vain of what ought rather to be felt than seen.

The humble, in the parable of the day of judgment, forgot their good works: "Lord, when did we so and so?"

He that does good for good's sake, seeks neither praise nor reward, though sure of both at last.

Complete Virtue

Content not thyself that thou art virtuous in the general; for, one link being wanting, the chain is defective.

Perhaps thou art rather innocent than virtuous, and owest more to thy constitution than to thy religion.

To be innocent, is to be not guilty; but to be virtuous, is to overcome our evil inclinations.

If thou hast not conquered thyself in that which is thy own particular weakness, thou hast no title to virtue, though thou art free of other men's.

For a covetous man to inveigh against prodigality, an atheist against idolatry, a tyrant against rebellion, or a liar against forgery, and a drunkard against intemperance, is vice reproving viciousness.

Such a reproof would have but little success, because it would carry but little authority with it.

If thou wouldst conquer thy weakness, thou must never gratify it.

No man is compelled to evil; his consent only makes it his.

It is no sin to be tempted, but to be overcome.

What man, in his right mind, would conspire his own hurt? Men are beside themselves when they transgress against their convictions.

If thou wouldst not sin, do not desire; and if thou wouldst not lust, do not embrace the temptation; no, not look at it, nor think of it.

Thou wouldst take much pains to save thy body; take some, prithee, to save thy soul.

Religion

Religion is the fear of God, and its demonstration good works; and faith is the root of both: "For without faith, we cannot please God;" nor can we fear what we do not believe.

The devils also believe and know abundance; but in this is the difference: their faith works not by love, nor their knowledge by obedience; and, therefore, they are never the better for them. And if ours be such, we shall be of their church, not of Christ's; for as the head is, so must the body be.

He was holy, humble, harmless, meek, merciful, &c., when among us, to teach us what we should be when he was gone; and yet he is among us still, and in us too, a living and perpetual preacher of the same grace, by his spirit in our consciences.

A minister of the Gospel ought to be one of Christ's making, if he would pass for one of Christ's ministers. And if he be one of his making, he knows and does, as well as believes.

That minister, whose life is not the model of his doctrine, is a babbler rather than a preacher, a quack rather than a physician of value.

Of old time, they were made ministers by the Holy Ghost; and the more that is an ingredient now, the fitter they are for that work.

Running streams are not so apt to corrupt as stagnant waters; nor itinerant as settled preachers; but they are not to run before they are sent.

As they freely receive from Christ, so they give.

They will not make that a trade, which they know ought not, in conscience, to be one.

Yet there is no fear of their living, that design not to live by it.

The humble and true teacher meets with more than he expects.

He accounts content with godliness great gain, and therefore seeks not to make a gain of godliness.

As the ministers of Christ are made by him, and are like him, so they beget people into the same likeness.

To be like Christ, then, is to be a Christian. And regeneration is the only way to the kingdom of God, which we pray for.

Let us to-day, therefore, hear his voice, and not harden our hearts, who speaks to us many ways: in the Scriptures, in our hearts, by his servants and providences; and the sum of all his holiness, and charity.

St. James gives a short draught of the matter, but very full and teaching: "Pure religion, and undefiled before God the Father, is this: to visit the fatherless and the widows in their afflictions, and to keep ourselves unspotted from the world;" which is comprised in these two words, charity and piety.

They that truly make these their aim, will find them their attainment; and with them, the peace that follows so excellent a condition.

Amuse not thyself, therefore, with the numerous opinions of the world; nor value thyself upon verbal orthodoxy, philosophy, or thy skill in tongues, or knowledge of the fathers, (too much the business and vanity of the world;) but in this rejoice, "That thou knowest God, that is the Lord, who exerciseth loving-kindness, and judgment, and righteousness in the earth."

Public worship is very commendable, if well performed. We owe it to God and good example. But we must know that God is not tied to time or place, who is every where at the same time; and this we shall know, as far as we are capable, if, wherever we are, our desires are to be with him.

Serving God, people generally confine to the acts of public and private worship; and those the more zealous do often repeat, in hopes of acceptance.

But if we consider that God is an infinite spirit, and, as such, every where; and that our Saviour has taught us that he will be worshipped in spirit and in truth, we shall see the shortness of such a notion.

For serving God concerns the frame of our spirits, in the whole course of our lives; in every occasion we have, in which we may show our love to his law.

For as men in battle are continually in the way of shot, so we in this world are ever within the reach of temptation; and herein do we serve God, if we avoid what we are forbid, as well as do what he commands.

God is better served in resisting a temptation to evil, than in many formal prayers.

This is but twice or thrice a day; but that every hour and moment of the day. So much more is our continual watch than our evening and morning devotion.

Wouldst thou, then, serve God? Do not that alone, which thou wouldst not that another should see thee do.

Do not take God's name in vain, nor disobey thy parents, nor wrong thy neighbor nor commit adultery, even in thy heart.

Neither be vain, lascivious, proud, drunken, revengeful, or angry; nor lie, detract, backbite, overreach, oppress, deceive, or betray; but watch vigorously against all temptation to these things, as knowing that God is present, the overseer of all thy ways and most inward thoughts, and the avenger of his own law upon the disobedient; and thou wilt acceptably serve God.

Is it not reason, if we expect the acknowledgments of those to whom we are bountiful, that we should reverently pay ours to God, our most munificent and constant benefactor?

The world represents a rare and sumptuous palace; mankind the great family in it; and God, the mighty Lord and Master of it. We are all sensible what a stately seat it is; the heavens adorned with so many glorious luminaries; and the earth with groves, plains, valleys, hills, fountains, ponds, lakes, and rivers, and variety of fruits and creatures for food, pleasure, and profit; in short, how noble a house he keeps, and the plenty, variety, and excellency of his table; his orders, seasons, and suitableness of every time and thing. But we must be as sensible, or at least ought to be, what careless and idle servants we are, and how short and disproportionable our behavior is to his bounty and goodness; how long he bears, how often he reprieves and forgives us; who, notwithstanding our breach of promises, and repeated neglects, has not yet been provoked to break up house, and send us to shift for ourselves. Should not this great goodness raise a due sense in us of our undutifulness, and a resolution to alter our course, and mend our manners; that we may be for the future more worthy communicants at our Maker's good and great table? Especially since it is not more certain that we deserve his displeasure, than that we shall feel it, if we continue to be unprofitable servants.

But though God has replenished this world with abundance of good things for man's life and comfort, yet they are all but imperfect goods. He only is the perfect good to whom they point. But alas! men cannot see him for them; though they should always see him in them.

I have often wondered at the unaccountableness of man in this, among other things; that, though he loves changes so well, he should care so little to hear or think of his last, great, and, if he pleases, his best, change.

Being, as to our bodies composed of changeable elements, we; with the world, are made up of, and subsist by revolution; but our souls being of another and nobler nature, we should seek our rest in a more enduring habitation.

The truest end of life is to know the life that never ends.

He that makes this his care will find it his crown at last.

Life else were a misery, rather than a pleasure; a judgment, not a blessing.

For, to know, regret, and resent, to desire, hope, and fear, more than a beast, and not live beyond him, is to make a man less than a beast.

It is the amends of a short and troublesome life, that doing good, and suffering ill, entitle man to one longer and better.

This ever raises the good man's hope, and gives him tastes beyond this world.

As it is his aim, so none else can hit the mark.

Many make it their speculation, but it is the good man's practice.

His work keeps pace with his life, and so leaves nothing to be done when he dies.

And he that lives to live for ever, never fears dying.

Nor can the means be terrible to him that heartily believes the end.

For though death be a dark passage, it leads to immortality; and that is recompense enough for suffering of it.

And yet faith lights us, even through the grave; being the evidence of things not seen.

And this is the comfort of the good, that the grave cannot hold them, and that they live as soon as they die.

For death is no more than a turning of us over from time to eternity.

Nor can there be a revolution without it; for it supposes the dissolution of one form, in order to the succession of another.

Death, then, being the way and condition of life, we cannot love to live, if we cannot bear to die.

Let us, then, not cozen ourselves with the shells and husks of things; nor prefer form to power, nor shadows to substance: pictures of bread will not satisfy hunger, nor those of devotion please God.

This world is a form; our bodies are forms; and no visible acts of devotion can be without forms. But yet the less form in religion the better, since God is a spirit: for the more mental our worship, the more adequate to the nature of God; the more silent, the more suitable to the language of a spirit.

Words are for others, not for ourselves: nor for God, who hears not as bodies do, but as spirits should.

If we would know this dialect, we must learn of the divine principle in us. As we hear the dictates of that, so God hears us.

There we may see him too in all his attributes; though but in little, yet as much as we can apprehend or bear: for as he is in himself, he is incomprehensible, and "dwelleth in that light no eye can approach." But in his image we may behold his glory: enough to exalt our apprehensions of God, and to instruct us in that worship which pleaseth him.

Men may tire themselves in a labyrinth of search, and talk of God; but if we would know him indeed, it must be from the impressions we receive of him: and the softer our hearts are, the deeper and livelier those will be upon us.

If he has made us sensible of his justice, by his reproof; of his patience, by his forbearance; of his mercy, by his forgiveness; of his holiness, by the sanctification of our hearts through his spirit; we have a grounded knowledge of God. This is experience, that speculation; this enjoyment, that report. In short, this is undeniable evidence, with the realities of religion, and will stand all winds and weathers.

As our faith, so our devotion, should be lively. Cold meat will not serve at those repasts.

It is a coal from God's altar must kindle our fire: and without fire, true fire, no acceptable sacrifice.

"Open thou my lips, and then" said the royal prophet, "my mouth shall praise God." But not till then.

The preparation of the heart, as well as the answer of the tongue, is of the Lord: and to have it, our prayers must be powerful, and our worship grateful.

Let us choose, therefore, to commune, where there is the warmest sense of religion; where devotion exceeds formality, and practice most corresponds with profession; and where there is, at least, as much charity as zeal: for where this society is to be found, there shall we find the church of God.

As good, so ill men, are all of a church: and every body knows who must be head of it.

The humble, meek, merciful, just, pious, and devout souls,

are every where of one religion; and when death has taken off the mask, they will know one another, though the diverse liveries they wear here make them strangers.

Great allowances are made for education and personal weaknesses; but it is a rule with me, 'That man is truly religious, that loves the persuasion he is of for the piety, rather than the ceremony, of it.'

They that have one end, can hardly disagree when they meet. At least their concern in the greater, moderates their value for, and difference about, the lesser things.

It is a sad reflection, that many men hardly have any religion at all, and most men have none of their own: for that which is the religion of their education, and not of their judgment, is the religion of another, and not theirs.

To have religion upon authority, and not upon conviction, is like a finger-watch, to be set forwards or backwards, as he pleases that has it in keeping.

It is a preposterous thing, that men can venture their souls, where they will not venture their money; for they will take their religion upon trust, but not trust a synod about the goodness of half a crown.

They will follow their own judgment when their money is concerned, whatever they do for their souls.

But, to be sure, that religion cannot be right, that a man is the worse for having.

No religion is better than an unnatural one.

Grace perfects, but never sours or spoils, nature.

To be unnatural in defence of grace is a contradiction.

Hardly any thing looks worse than to defend religion by ways that shew it has no credit with us.

A devout man is one thing, a stickler is quite another.

When our minds exceed their just bounds, we must not discredit what we would recommend.

To be furious in religion is to be irreligiously religious.

If he that is without bowels is not a man; how, then, can he be a Christian?

It were better to be of no church, than to be bitter for any.

Bitterness comes very near to enmity, and that is Beelzebub; because the perfection of wickedness.

A good end cannot sanctify evil means; nor must we ever do evil that good may come of it.

Some folks think they may scold, rail, hate, rob, and kill too; so it be but for God's sake.

But nothing in us unlike him can please him.

It is a great presumption to send our passions upon God's errands, as it is to palliate them with God's name.

Zeal dropped in charity, is good; without it, good for nothing: for it devours all it comes near.

They may first judge themselves, that presume to censure others; and such will not be apt to over-shoot the mark.

We are too ready to retaliate, rather than forgive, or gain by love and information.

And yet we could hurt no man that we believe loves us.

Let us, then, try what love will do: for if men do once see that we love them, we should soon find they would not harm us.

Force may subdue, but love gains; and he that forgives first, wins the laurel.

If I am even with my enemy, the debt is paid; but if I forgive it, I oblige him for ever.

Love is the hardest lesson in christianity; but, for that reason, it should be most our care to learn it. 'Difficilia quæ pulchra.'

It is a severe rebuke upon us, that God makes us so many allowances, and we make so few to our neighbor: as if charity had nothing to do with religion; or love with faith, that ought to work by it.

I find all sorts of people agree, whatsoever were their animosities, when humbled by the approaches of death; then they forgive, then they pray for, and love one another: which shows us, that it is not our reason, but our passion, that makes and holds up the feuds that reign among men in their health and fulness. They, therefore, that live nearest to that state in which they should die, must certainly live the best.

Did we believe a final reckoning and judgment, or did we think enough of what we do believe, we should allow more love in religion than we do: since religion itself is nothing else but love to God and man.

"He that lives in love, lives in God," says the beloved disciple: and, to be sure, a man can live no where better.

It is most reasonable men should value that benefit which is most durable. Now tongues shall cease, and prophecy fail, and faith shall be consummated in sight, and hope in enjoyment; but love remains.

Love is indeed heaven upon earth; since heaven above would not be heaven without it; for where there is not love, there is fear; but, "Perfect love casts out fear." And yet we naturally fear most to offend what we most love.

What we love, we will hear; what we love, we will trust: and what we love, we will serve, aye, and suffer for too. "If you love me," says our blessed Redeemer, "keep my commandments." Why? Why then, he will love us: then we shall be his friends; then he will send us the Comforter; then whatever we ask we shall receive; and then, where he is we shall be also, and that for ever. Behold, the fruits of love; the power, virtue, benefit, and beauty of love!

Love is above all; and when it prevails in us all, we shall all be lovely, and in love with God, and one with another. Amen.

The Right Moralist

A right moralist is a great and good man; but for that reason, he is rarely to be found.

There are a sort of people that are fond of the character, who, in my opinion, have but little title to it.

They think it enough, not to defraud a man of his pay, or betray his friend; but never consider, that the law forbids the one at his peril, and that virtue is seldom the reason of the other.

But certainly, he that covets can no more be a moral man, than he that steals; since he does it so in his mind. Nor can he be one that robs his neighbor of his credit, or that craftily undermines him of his trade or office.

If a man pays his tailor, but debauches his wife, is he a current moralist?

But what shall we say of the man that rebels against his father, is an ill husband, or an abusive neighbor; one that is lavish of his time, of his health, and of his estate, in which his family is so nearly concerned? Must he go for a right moralist, because he pays his rent well?

I would ask some of those men of morals, whether he that robs God, and himself too, though he should not defraud his neighbor, be the moral man?

Do I owe myself nothing? And do I not owe all to God? And if paying what we owe makes the moral man, is it not fit we should begin to render our dues where we owe our very beginning; aye, our all?

The complete moralist begins with God; he gives him his due, his heart, his love, his service: the bountiful giver of his well-being, as well as being.

He that lives without a sense of this dependence and obligation, cannot be a moral man, because he does not know his returns of love and obedience, as becomes an honest and sensible creature: which very term implies he is not his own; and it cannot be very honest to misemploy another's goods.

But now! can there be no debt to a fellow creature? Or, will our exactness in paying those trifling ones, while we neglect our weightier obligations, cancel the bonds we lie under, and render us right and thorough moralists?

As judgments are paid before bonds, and bonds before bills or book-debts; so the moralist considers his obligations according to their several dignities. In the first place, him to whom he owes himself. Next, himself, in his health and livelihood. Lastly, his other obligations, whether rational or pecuniary; doing to others, to the extent of his ability, as he would have them do unto him.

In short, the moral man is he that loves God above all, and his neighbor as himself; which fulfils both tables at once.

The World's Able Man

It is by some thought the character of an able man, to be dark, and not understood. But I am sure that is not fair play.

If he be so by silence, it is better; but if by disguises, it is insincere and hateful.

Secrecy is one thing, false lights are another.

The honest man that is rather free than open, is ever to be preferred; especially when sense is at the helm.

The glorying of the other humor is in a vice: for it is not human to be cold, dark, and unconversable. I was going to say, they are like pick-pockets in a crowd, where a man must ever have his hand on his purse: or as spies in a garrison, that, if not prevented, betray it.

They are the reverse of human nature; and yet this is the present world's wise man and politician.

Like highwaymen, that rarely rob without vizard's, or in the same wigs and clothes, but have a dress for every enterprise.

At best, he may be a cunning man, which is a sort of lurcher in politics.

He is never too hard for the wise man upon the square; for that is out of his element, and puts him quite by his skill. Nor are wise men ever catched by him, but when they trust him.

But as cold and close as he seems, he can and will please all, if he gets by it; though it should neither please God nor himself at bottom.

He is for every cause that brings him gain; but implacable, if disappointed of success.

And what he cannot hinder, he will be sure to spoil by overdoing it.

None are so zealous then as he, for that which he cannot abide.

What is it he will not, or cannot do, to hide his true sentiments?

For his interest he refuses no side or party; and will take the wrong by the hand, when the other will not do, with as good a grace as the right.

Nay, he commonly chooses the worst, because that brings the best bribe; his cause being ever money.

He sails with all winds, and is never out of his way, where any thing is to be had.

A privateer, indeed, and every where a bird of prey.

True to nothing but himself: and false to all persons and parties, to serve his own turn.

Talk with him as often as you please, he will never pay you in good coin; for it is either false or clipped.

But to give a false reason for any thing, let my reader never learn of him, no more than to give a brass half crown for a good one: not only because it is not true, but because it deceives the person to whom it is given: which I take to be an immorality.

Silence is much preferable; for it saves the secret, as well as the person's honor.

Such as give themselves the latitude of saying what they do not mean, come to be arrant jockeys at more things than one: but in religion and politics it is pernicious.

To hear two men talk the reverse of their own sentiments, with all the good breeding and appearance of friendship imaginable, on purpose to cozen or pump each other, is, to a man of virtue and honor, one of the most melancholy, as well as most nauseous things in the world.

But that it should be the character of an able man, is to disinherit wisdom, and paint out our degeneracy to the life, by setting up fraud, an arrant impostor, in her room.

The trial of skill between these two is, who shall believe least of what the other says; and he that has the weakness or good nature, to give out first (viz. to believe any thing the other says) is looked upon to be tricked.

I cannot see the policy, any more than the necessity, of a man's mind giving the lie to his mouth; or his mouth giving false alarms of his mind: for no man can be long believed, that teaches all men to distrust him; and since the ablest have sometimes need of credit, where lies the advantage of their politic cant or banter upon mankind?

I remember a passage of one of Queen Elizabeth's great men, as advice to his friend: "The advantage," says he, "I had upon others at court, was, that I always spoke as I thought; which being not believed by them, I both preserved a good conscience, and suffered no damage from that freedom:" which, as it shows the vice to be older than our times, so does it that gallant man's integrity to be the best way of avoiding it.

To be sure it is wise, as well as honest, neither to flatter other men's sentiments, nor dissemble, and less to contradict, our own.

To hold one's tongue, or to speak truth, or talk only of indifferent things, is the fairest conversation.

Woman that rarely go abroad without vizard masks, have none of the best reputation. But when we consider what all this art and disguise are for, it equally heightens the wise man's wonder and aversion; perhaps it is to betray a father, a brother, a master, a friend, a neighbor, or one's own party.

A fine conquest! what noble Grecians and Romans abhorred; as if government could not subsist without knavery, and that knaves were the most useful props to it; though the basest, as well as greatest, perversions of the ends of it.

But that it should become a maxim, shows but too grossly the corruptions of the times.

I confess I have heard the style of 'An useful knave,' but ever took it to be a silly or a knavish saying; at least, an excuse of knavery.

It is as reasonable to think a loose woman makes the best wife, as a knave the best officer.

Beside, employing knaves encourages knavery, instead of punishing it, and alienates the reward of virtue; or at least, must make the world believe the country yields not honest men enough, able to serve her.

Art thou a magistrate? Prefer such as have clean characters where they live; and men of estates to secure a just discharge of their trusts, that are under no temptation to strain points for a fortune: for sometimes such may be found sooner than they are employed.

Art thou a private man? Contract thy acquaintance on a narrow compass, and choose those for the subjects of it that are men of principle; such as will make full stops, where honor will not lead them on: and that had rather bear the disgrace of not being thorough paced men, than forfeit their peace and reputation by a base compliance.

The Wise Man

The wise man governs himself by the reason of his case, and because what he does is best: best, in a moral and prudent, not a sinister sense.

He proposes just ends, and employs the fairest and most probable means and methods to attain them.

Though you cannot always penetrate his design, or his reasons for it, yet you shall ever see his actions of a piece, and his performance like a workman: they will bear the touch of wisdom and honor, as often as they are tried.

He scorns to serve himself by indirect means, or to be an interloper in government; since just enterprises never want any unjust ways to make them succeed.

To do evil that good may come of it, is for bunglers, in politics as well as morals.

Like those surgeons that will cut off an arm that they cannot cure, to hide their ignorance and save their credit.

The wise man is cautious, but not cunning; judicious, but not crafty; making virtue the measure of using his excellent understanding in the conduct of his life.

The wise man is equal, ready, but not officious; has in every thing an eye to sure-footing: he offends no body, nor is easily offended; and is always willing to compound for wrongs, if not forgive them.

He is never captious nor critical; hates banter and jests; he may be pleasant but not light; he never deals but in substantial ware, and leaves the rest for the toy pates (or shops) of the world; which are so far from being his business, that they are not so much as his diversion.

He is always for some solid good, civil or moral: as to make his country more virtuous, preserve her peace and liberty, employ her poor, improve land, advance trade, suppress vice, encourage industry, and all mechanical knowledge; and that they should be the care of the government, and the blessing and praise of the people.

To conclude, he is just, and fears God, hates covetousness, and eschews evil, and loves his neighbor as himself.

Of the Government of Thoughts

Man being made a reasonable, and so a thinking creature, there is nothing more worthy of his being, than the right direction and employment of his thoughts: since upon this depends both his usefulness to the public, and his own present and future benefit in all respects.

The consideration of this has often obliged me to lament the unhappiness of mankind, that, through too great a mixture and confusion of thoughts, have hardly been able to make a right or mature judgment of things.

To this is owing the various uncertainty and confusion we see in the world, and the intemperate zeal that occasions them.

To this, also is to be attributed the imperfect knowledge we have of things, and the slow progress we make in attaining to a better: like the children of Israel, that were forty years upon their journey from Egypt to Canaan, which might have been performed in less than one.

In fine, it is to this we ought to ascribe, if not all, at least most of the infelicities we labor under.

Clear, therefore, thy head, and rally and manage thy thoughts rightly, and thou wilt save time, and see and do thy business well: for thy judgment will be distinct, thy mind free, and thy faculties strong and regular.

Always remember to bound thy thoughts to the present occasion.

If it be thy religious duty, suffer nothing else to share in them. And if any civil or temporal affair, observe the same caution, and, thou wilt be a whole man to every thing, and do twice the business in the same time.

If any point over-labors thy mind, divert and relieve it by some other subject, of a more sensible or manual nature, rather than what may affect the understanding: for this were to write one thing upon another, which blots out our former impressions, or render them illegible.

They that are least divided in their care, always give the best account of their business.

As, therefore, thou art always to pursue the present subject till thou hast mastered it, so if it fall out that thou hast more affairs than one upon thy hands, be sure to prefer that which is of most moment, and will least wait thy leisure.

He that judges not well of the importance of his affairs, though he may be always busy, must make but a small progress.

But make not more business necessary than is so; rather lessen than augment work for thyself.

Nor yet be over eager in the pursuit of any thing; for the mercurial too often happen to leave judgment behind them, and sometimes make work for repentance.

He that over-runs his business, leaves it for him that follows more leisurely to take it up: which has often proved a profitable harvest to them that never sowed.

It is the advantage that slower tempers have upon the men of lively parts, that though they do not lead, they will follow well, and glean clean.

Upon the whole matter, employ thy thoughts as thy business requires, and let that have place according to merit and urgency, giving every thing a review and due digestion; and thou wilt prevent many errors and vexations, as well as save much time to thyself in the course of thy life.

Of Envy

It is the mark of ill nature, to lessen good actions, and aggravate ill ones.

Some men do as much begrudge others a good name, as they want one themselves: and perhaps that is the reason of it.

But certainly they are in the wrong that can think they are lessened, because others have their due.

Such people generally have less merit than ambition, that covet the reward of other men's; and, to be sure, a very ill nature, that will rather rob others of their due, than allow them their praise.

It is more an error of our will than our judgment; for we know it to be an effect of our passion, not our reason; and therefore we are the more culpable in our partial estimates.

It is as envious as unjust, to underrate another's actions, where their intrinsic worth recommends them to disengaged minds.

Nothing shows more the folly, as well as fraud of man, than clipping merit and reputation.

And as some men think it an alloy to themselves, that others have their right; so they know no end of pilfering, to raise their own credit.

This envy is the child of pride; and mis-gives rather than mistakes.

It will have charity to be ostentation; sobriety, covetousness; humility, craft; bounty, popularity. In short, virtue must be design, and religion only interest. Nay, the best of qualities must not pass without a 'but' to alloy their merit, and abate their praise. Basest of tempers! and they that have it, the worst of men.

But just and noble minds rejoice in other men's success and help to augment their praise.

And, indeed they are not without a love to virtue, that take a satisfaction in seeing her rewarded, and such deserve to share her character, that do abhor to lessen it.

Of Man's Life

Why is man less durable than the works of his hands, but because this is not the place of his rest.

And it is a great and just reproach upon him, that he should fix his mind where he cannot stay himself.

Were it not more his wisdom to be concerned about those works that will go with him, and erect a mansion for him, where time has power neither over him nor it?

It is a sad thing for a man so often to miss his way to his best, as well as most lasting home.

Of Ambition

They that soar too high, often fall hard; which makes a low and level dwelling preferable.

The tallest trees are most in the power of the winds; and ambitious men of the blasts of fortune.

They are most seen and observed, and most envied; least quiet, but most talked of, and not often to their advantage.

Those buildings had need of a good foundation, that lie so much exposed to weather.

Good works are a rock that will support their credit; but ill ones, a sandy foundation, that yields to calamities.

And truly they ought to expect no pity in their fall, who, when in power, had no bowels for the unhappy.

The worst of distempers; always craving and thirsty, restless and hated; a perfect delirium in the mind; insufferable in success, and in disappointments most revengeful.

Of Praise or Applause

We are apt to love praise, but not to deserve it.

But if we would deserve it, we must love virtue more than that.

As there is no passion in us sooner moved, or more deceivable, so, for that reason, there is none over which we ought to be more watchful, whether we give or receive it: for if we give it, we must be sure to mean it, and measure it too.

If we are penurious it shows emulation; if we exceed, flattery.

Good measure belongs to good actions; more, looks nauseous, as well as insincere: besides, it is persecuting the meritorious, who is out of countenance to hear what he deserves.

It is much easier for him to merit applause, than hear of it: and he never doubts himself more, or the person that gives it, than when he hears so much of it.

But, to say true, there need not many cautions on this hand; since the world is rarely just enough to the deserving.

However, we cannot be too circumspect how we receive praise: for if we contemplate ourselves in a false glass, we are sure to be mistaken about our dues: and because we are too apt to believe what is pleasing, rather than what is true, we may be too easily swelled beyond our just proportion, by the windy compliments of men.

Make ever, therefore, allowances for what is said on such occasions; or thou exposest, as well as deceivest thyself.

For an over value of ourselves, gives us but a dangerous security in many respects.

We expect more than belongs to us; take all that is given us, though never meant us; and fall out with those that are not so full of us as we are of ourselves.

In short, it is a passion that abuses our judgment, and makes us both unsafe and ridiculous.

Be not fond, therefore, of praise; but seek virtue that leads to it.

And yet no more lessen or dissemble thy merit, than over-rate it; for, though humility be a virtue, an affected one is none.

Of Conduct in Speech

Inquire often, but judge rarely, and thou wilt not often be mistaken.

It is safer to learn than to teach; and he who conceals his opinion has nothing to answer for.

Vanity or resentment often engages us, and it is two to one but we come off losers; for one shows a want of judgment and humility, as the other does of temper and discretion.

Not that I admire the reserved; for they are next to unnatural that are not communicable. But if reservedness be at any time a virtue, it is in throngs, or ill company.

Beware also of affectation in speech: it often wrongs matter, and ever shows a blind side.

Speak properly, and in as few words as you can, but always plainly: for the end of speech is not ostentation, but to be understood.

They that affect words more than matter will dry up that little they have.

Sense never fails to give them that have it, words enough to make themselves understood.

But it too often happens in some conversations, as in apothecaries' shops, that those pots that are empty, or have things of small value in them, are as gaudily dressed and flourished as those that are full of precious drugs.

This laboring of slight matter with flourished turns of expression is fulsome; and worse than the modern imitation of tapestry, and East-India goods, in stuffs and linens. In short, it is but tawdry talk, and next to very trash.

Union of Friends

They that love beyond the world cannot be separated by it.

Death cannot kill what never dies.

Nor can spirits ever be divided, that love and live in the same divine principle, the root and record, of their friendship.

If absence be not death, neither is theirs.

Death is but crossing the world, as friends do the seas; they live in one another still.

For they must needs be present that love and live in that which is omnipresent.

In this divine glass they see face to face; and their converse is free as well as pure.

This is the comfort of friends, that though they may be said to die, yet their friendship and society are, in the best sense, ever present, because immortal.

On Being Easy in Living

It is a happiness to be delivered from a curious mind, as well as from a dainty palate.

For it is not only a troublesome but slavish thing to be nice.

They narrow their own freedom and comforts, that make so much requisite to enjoy them.

To be easy in living is much of the pleasure of life; but difficult tempers will always want it.

A careless and homely breeding is therefore preferable to one nice and delicate.

And he that is taught to live upon little, owes more to his father's wisdom, than he that has a great deal left him, does to his father's care.

Children cannot well be too hardily bred: for besides that it fits them to bear the roughest providences, it is more active and healthy.

Nay, it is certain, that the liberty of the mind is mightily preserved by it; for so it is served, instead of being a servant, indeed a slave, to sensual delicacies.

As nature is soon answered, so are such satisfied.

The memory of the ancients is hardly in any thing more to be celebrated, than in a strict and useful instruction of youth.

By labor they prevented luxury in their young people, till wisdom and philosophy had taught them to resist and despise it.

It must be therefore a gross fault to strive so hard for the pleasure of our bodies, and be so insensible and careless of the freedom of our souls.

Of Man's Inconsiderateness and Partiality

It is very observable, if our civil rights are invaded or encroached upon, we are mightily touched, and fill every place with our resentment and complaint; while we suffer ourselves, our better and nobler selves, to be the property and vassals of sin, the worst of invaders.

In vain do we expect to be delivered from such troubles, till we are delivered from the cause of them, our disobedience to God.

When he has his dues from us, it will be time enough for him to give us ours out of one another.

It is our great happiness if we could understand it, that we meet with such checks in the career of our worldly enjoyments; lest we should forget the giver, adore the gift, and terminate our felicity here, which is not man's ultimate bliss.

Our losses are often made judgments by our guilt, and mercies by our repentance.

Besides, it argues great folly in men to let their satisfaction exceed the true value of any temporal matter: for disappointments are not always to be measured by the loss of the thing, but the overvalue we put upon it.

And thus men improve their own miseries, for want of an equal and just estimate of what they enjoy or lose.

There lies a proviso upon every thing in this world, and we must observe it at our own peril, viz. to love God above all, and act for judgment; the last I mean.

Of the Rule of Judging

In all things reason should prevail: it is quite another thing to be stiff, than steady in an opinion.

This may be reasonable, but that is ever wilful.

In such cases, it always happens, that the clearer the argument, the greater the obstinacy, where the design is not to be convinced.

This is to value humor more than truth, and prefer a sullen pride to a reasonable submission.

It is the glory of a man to vail to truth; as it is the mark of a good nature to be easily entreated.

Beasts act by sense, man should act by reason; else he is a greater beast than ever God made: and the proverb is verified,

"The corruption of the best things is the worst and most offensive."

A reasonable opinion must ever be in danger where reason is not judge.

Though there is a regard due to education, and the tradition of our fathers, truth will ever deserve, as well as claim the preference.

If, like Theophilus and Timothy, we have been brought up in the knowledge of the best things, it is our advantage; but neither they nor we lose by trying the truth; for so we learn their, as well as its, intrinsic worth.

Truth never lost ground by inquiry, because she is, most of all, reasonable.

Nor can that need another authority that is self-evident.

If my own reason be on the side of a principle, with what can I dispute or withstand it?

And if men would once consider one another reasonably, they would either reconcile their differences, or maintain them more amicably.

Let that, therefore, be the standard, that has most to say for itself: though of that let every man be judge for himself.

Reason, like the sun, is common to all: and it is for want of examining all by the same light and measure, that we are not all of the same mind: for all have it to that end, though all do not use it so.

Of Formality

Form is good, but not formality.

In the use of the best of forms there is too much of that I fear.

It is absolutely necessary, that this distinction should go along with people in their devotion; for too many are apter to rest upon what they do, than how they do their duty.

If it were considered, that it is the frame of the mind that gives our performances acceptance, we would lay more stress on our inward preparation than our outward action.

Of the Mean Notions We Have of God

Nothing more shows the low condition man is fallen into, than the unsuitable notion we must have of God, by the ways we take to please him.

As if it availed any thing to him, that we performed so many ceremonies and external forms of devotion; who never meant more by them than to try our obedience, and through them, to show us something more excellent and durable beyond them.

Doing, while we are undoing, is good for nothing.

Of what benefit is it to say our prayers regularly, go to church, receive the sacrament, and may be, go to confessions too; aye, feast the priest, and give alms to the poor; and yet lie, swear, curse, be drunk, covetous, unclean, proud, revengeful, vain, or idle, at the same time.

Can one excuse or balance the other? Or will God think himself well served, where his law is violated? Or well used where there is so much more show than substance?

It is a most dangerous error, for a man to think to excuse himself in the breach of a moral duty, by a formal performance of positive worship; and less, when of human invention.

Our blessed Saviour most rightly and clearly distinguished and determined this case, when he told the Jew, "That they were his mother, his brethren, and sisters, who did the will of his Father."

Of the Benefit of Justice

Justice is a great support of society, because an insurance to all men of their property: this violated, there is no security: which throws all into confusion to recover it.

An honest man is a fast pledge in dealing. A man is sure to have it, if it be to be had.

Many are so, merely of necessity; others not so only for the same reason; but such an honest man is not to be thanked: and such a dishonest man is to be pitied.

But he that is dishonest for gain, is next to a robber, and to be punished for example.

And, indeed, there are few dealers but what are faulty; which makes trade difficult, and a great temptation to men of virtue.

It is not what they should, but what they can get: faults or decays must be concealed, big words given where they are not deserved, and the ignorance or necessity of the buyer imposed upon, for unjust profit.

These are the men that keep their words for their own ends; and are only just for fear of the magistrate.

A politic rather than a moral honesty; a constrained, not a chosen justice; according to the proverb, "Patience per force, and thank you for nothing."

But of all injustice, that is the greatest that passes under the name of law. A cut-purse in Westminster-Hall exceeds; for that advances injustice to oppression, where law is alleged for that which it should punish.

Of Jealousy

The jealous are troublesome to others, but a torment to themselves.

Jealousy is a kind of civil war in the soul, where judgment and imagination are at perpetual jars.

This civil dissension in the mind, like that of the body politic, commits great disorders and lays all waste.

Nothing stands safe in its way: nature, interest, religion, must yield to its fury.

It violates contracts, dissolves society, breaks wedlock, betrays friends and neighbors: no body is good, and every one is either doing or designing them a mischief.

It has a venom that more or less rankles wherever it bites: and as it reports fancies for facts, so it disturbs its own house, as often as other folks.

Its rise is guilt or ill-nature; and by reflection it thinks its own faults to be other men's; as he that is overrun with the jaundice takes others to be yellow.

A jealous man only sees his own spectrum when he looks upon other men, and gives his character in theirs.

Of State

I love service, but not state: one is useful, the other superfluous.

The trouble of this, as well as charge, is real; but the advantage only imaginary.

Besides, it helps to set us up above ourselves, and augments our temptation to disorder.

The least thing out of joint, or omitted, makes us uneasy; and we are ready to think ourselves ill served about that which is of no real service at all; or so much better than other men, as we have the means of greater state.

But this is all for want of wisdom, which carries the truest and most forcible state along with it.

He that makes not himself cheap by indiscreet conversation, puts value enough upon himself every where.

The other is rather pageantry than state.

Of a Good Servant

A true, and a good servant, are the same thing.

But no servant is true to his master that defrauds him.

Now there are many ways of defrauding a master, as, of time, care, pains, respect, and reputation, as well as money.

He that neglects his work, robs his master, since he is fed and paid as if he did his best: and he that is not as diligent in the absence as in the presence of his master, cannot be a true servant.

Nor is he a true servant that buys dear to share in the profit with the seller.

Nor yet he that tells tales without doors; or deals basely, in his master's name, with other people; or connives at other's loiterings, wastings, or dishonorable reflections.

So that a true servant is diligent, secret, and respectful; more tender of his master's honor and interest, than of his own profit.

Such a servant deserves well; and, if modest under his merit, should liberally feel it at his master's hand.

Of an Immoderate Pursuit of the World

It shows a depraved state of mind, to cark and care for that which one does not need.

Some are as eager to be rich, as ever they were to live; for superfluity, as for subsistence.

But that plenty should augment covetousness, is a perversion of providence; and yet the generality are the worse for their riches.

But it is strange that old men should excel; for generally money lies nearest them, that are the nearest their graves; as if they would augment their love, in proportion to the little time they have left to enjoy it: and yet their pleasure is without enjoyment, since none enjoy what they do not use.

So that instead of learning to leave their great wealth easily, they hold it the faster, because they must leave it: so sordid is the temper of some men.

Where charity keeps pace with gain, industry is blessed: but to slave to get, and keep it sordidly, is a sin, against providence, a vice in government, and an injury to their neighbors.

Such as they, spend not one fifth of their income; and, it may be, give not one tenth of what they spend to the needy.

This is the worst sort of idolatry, because there can be no religion in it, nor ignorance pleaded in excuse of it; and that it wrongs other folks that ought to share therein.

Of the Interest of the Public in Our Estates

Hardly any thing is given us for ourselves, but the public may claim a share with us. But of all we call ours, we are most accountable to God, and the public, for our estates: in this we are but stewards: and to hoard up all to ourselves is great injustice, as well as ingratitude.

If all men were so far tenants to the public, that the superfluities of gain and expense were applied to the exigencies thereof, it would put an end to taxes, leave not a beggar, and make the greatest bank for national trade in Europe.

It is a judgment upon us, as well as weakness, though we will not see it, to begin at the wrong end.

If the taxes we give are not to maintain pride, I am sure there would be less, if pride were made a tax to the government.

I confess I have wondered that so many lawful and useful things are exercised by laws, and pride left to reign free over them and the public.

But, since people are more afraid of the laws of man than of God, because their punishment seems to be nearest, I know not how magistrates can be excused in their suffering such excess with impunity.

Our noble English patriarchs, as well as patriots, were so sensible of this evil, that they made several excellent laws, commonly called sumptuary, to forbid, at least limit, the pride of the people; and, because the execution of them would be our interest and honor, their neglect must be our just reproach and loss.

It is but reasonable that the punishment of pride and excess should help to support the government; since it must otherwise inevitably be ruined by them.

But some say, "It ruins trade, and will make the poor burdensome to the public:" but if such trade, in consequence, ruins the kingdom, is it not time to ruin that trade? Is moderation no part of our duty; and is temperance an enemy to government.

He is a Judas, that will get money by any thing.

To wink at a trade that effeminates the people, and invades the ancient discipline of the kingdom, is a crime capital, and to be severely punished, instead of being excused by the magistrate.

Is there no better employment for the poor than luxury? Miserable nation!

What did they before they fell into these forbidden methods? Is there not land enough in England to cultivate, and more and better manufactories to be made?

Have we no room for them in our plantations, about things that may augment trade, without luxury?

In short, let pride pay, and excess be well excised; and if that will not cure the people, it will help to keep the kingdom.

The Vain Man

But a vain man is a nauseous creature: he is so full of himself, that he has no room for any thing else, be it ever so good or deserving.

It is I, at every turn, that does this, or can do that. And as he abounds in his comparisons, so he is sure to give himself the better of every body else: according to the proverb, "All his geese are swans."

They are certainly to be pitied that can be so much mistaken at home.

And yet I have sometimes thought, that such people are, in a sort, happy, that nothing can put out of countenance with themselves, though they neither have nor merit other people's.

But, at the same time, one would wonder they should not feel the blows they give themselves, or get from others, for this intolerable and ridiculous temper; nor show any concern at that, which makes others blush for, as well as at them; viz. their unreasonable assurance.

To be a man's own fool is bad enough; but the vain man is every body's.

This silly disposition comes of a mixture of ignorance, confidence and pride; and as there is more or less of the last, so it is more or less offensive, or entertaining.

And yet, perhaps the worst part of this vanity is its unteachableness. Tell it any thing, and it has known it long ago; and outruns information and instruction, or else proudly puffs at it.

Whereas the greatest understandings doubt most, are readiest to learn, and least pleased with themselves; this, with nobody else.

For though they stand on higher ground, and so see farther than their neighbors, they are yet humbled by their prospect, since it shows them something so much higher, and above their reach.

And truly then it is that sense shines with the greatest beauty, when it is set in humility.

An humble able man is a jewel worth a kingdom; it is often saved by him, as Solomon's poor wise man did the city.

May we have more of them or less need of them.

The Conformist

It is reasonable to concur, where conscience does not forbid compliance; for conformity is at least a civil virtue.

But we should only press it in necessaries; the rest may prove a snare or temptation to break society.

But, above all, it is a weakness in religion and government, where it is carried to things of an indifferent nature; since, besides that it makes way for scruples, liberty is always the price of it.

Such conformists have little to boast of, and therefore the less reason to reproach others that have more latitude.

And yet the latitudinarian that I love, is one that is only so in charity: for the freedom I recommend is no scepticism in judgment, and much less so in practice.

The Obligations of Great Men
to Almighty God

It seems but reasonable that those whom God has distinguished from others by his goodness, should distinguish themselves to him by their gratitude.

For though he has made of one blood all nations, he has not ranged or dignified them upon the level, but in a sort of subordination and dependency.

If we look upwards, we find it in the heavens, where the planets have their several degrees of glory; and so the other stars, of magnitude and lustre.

If we look upon the earth, we see it among the trees of the wood, from the cedar to the bramble; among the fishes, from the leviathan to the sprat; in the air, among the birds, from the eagle to the sparrow; among the beasts, from the lion to the cat; and among mankind, from the king to the scavenger.

Our great men, doubtless, were designed, by the wise framer of the world, for our religious, moral, and politic planets; for lights and directions to the lower ranks of the numerous company of their own kind, both in precepts and examples; and they are well paid for their pains too, who have the honor and service of their fellow creatures, and the marrow and fat of the earth for their share.

But is it not a most unaccountable folly, that men should be proud of the providences that should humble them? or think the better of themselves, instead of him who raised them so much above the level; or of being so in their lives, in return for his extraordinary favors?

But it is but too near akin to us, to think no further than ourselves either in the acquisition, or use, of our wealth and greatness; when, alas! they are the preferments of Heaven, to try our wisdom, bounty and gratitude.

It is a dangerous perversion of the end of providence, to consume the time, power, and wealth, he has given us above other men, to gratify our sordid passions, instead of playing the good stewards, to the honor of our great benefactor, and the good of our fellow creatures.

But it is an injustice, too; since those higher ranks of men are but the trustees of Heaven, for the benefit of lesser mortals: who as minors, are entitled to all their care and provision.

For though God has dignified some men above their brethren, it never was to serve their pleasures; but that they might take pleasure to serve the public.

For this cause, doubtless, it was that they were raised above necessity, or any trouble to live, that they might have more time and ability to care for others: and it is certain, where that use is not made of the bounties of providence, they are embezzled and wasted.

If has often struck me with a serious reflection, when I have observed the great inequality of the world; that one man should have such numbers of his fellow creatures to wait upon him, who have souls to be saved as well as he; and this not for business, but state. Certainly a poor employment of his money, and a worse of their time.

But that any one man should make work for so many, or rather keep them from work to make up a train, has a levity or luxury in it very reprovable, both in religion and government.

But even in allowable services, it has an humbling consideration, and what should raise the thankfulness of the great men to him who so much bettered their circumstances; and moderate the use of their dominion over those of their own kind.

When the poor Indians hear us call any of our family by the name of servants, they cry out, "What! call brethren servants! we call our dogs servants, but never men." The moral certainly can do us no harm, but may instruct us to abate our height and narrow our state and attendance.

And what has been said of their excess may, in some measure, be applied to other branches of luxury, that set ill examples to the lesser world, and rob the needy of their pensions.

God Almighty touch the hearts of our grandees with a sense of his distinguished goodness, and the true end of it; that they may better distinguish themselves in their conduct, to the glory of Him that has thus liberally preferred them, and to the benefit of their fellow creatures!

Of Refining Upon Other Men's Actions or Interests

This seems to be the master piece of our politicians; but nobody shoots more at random than those refiners.

A perfect lottery, and mere hazard! since the true spring of the actions of men is as invisible as their hearts; and so are the thoughts too, of their several interests.

He that judges of other men by himself, does not always hit the mark: because all men have not the same capacity, nor passions in interest.

If any able man refines upon the proceedings of an ordinary capacity, according to his own, he must ever miss it: but much more the ordinary man, when he shall pretend to speculate the motives to the able man's actions; for the able man deceives himself by making the other wiser than he is in the reason of his conduct; and the ordinary man makes himself so, in presuming to judge of the reasons of the abler man's actions.

It is, in short, a word, a maze; and of nothing are we more uncertain, nor in any thing do we oftener befool ourselves.

The mischiefs are many that follow this humor, and dangerous: for men misguide themselves, act upon false measures, and meet frequently with mischievous disappointments.

It excludes all confidence in commerce; allows of no such thing as a principle in practice; supposes every man to act upon other reasons than what appear; and that there is no such thing as uprightness or sincerity among mankind: a trick, instead of truth.

Neither allowing nature, or religion, but some worldly turn or advantage, to be the true, the hidden motive of all men.

It is hard to express its uncharitableness, as well as uncertainty; and has more of vanity than benefit in it.

This foolish quality gives a large field; but let what I have said serve, for this time.

Of Charity

Charity has various senses, but is excellent in all of them.

It imparts, first, the commiseration of the poor and unhappy of mankind, and extends a helping hand to mend their condition.

They that feel nothing of this are, at best, not above half of kin to the human race; since they must have no bowels, which make such an essential part thereof, who have no more nature.

A man! and yet not have the feeling of the wants or needs of his own flesh and blood! a monster rather! and may he never be suffered to propagate such an unnatural stock in the world!

Such an uncharitableness spoils the best gains; and two to one but it entails a curse upon the possessors.

Nor can we expect to be heard of God in our prayers, that turn the deaf ear to the petitions of the distressed among our fellow creatures.

God sends the poor to try us; as well as he tries them by being such: and he that refuses them a little, out of the great deal that God has given him, lays up poverty in store for his own posterity.

I will not say these works are meritorious, but I dare say they are acceptable, and go not without their reward; though, to humble us in our fulness, and liberality too, we only give what is given us to give, as well as to use: for if we ourselves are not our own, less is that so which God has intrusted us with.

Next, charity makes the best construction of things and persons; and is so far from being an evil spy, a backbiter, or a detractor, that it excuses weakness, extenuates miscarriages, makes the best of every thing, forgives every body, serves all, and hopes to the end.

It moderates extremes, is always for expedients, labors to accommodate differences, and had rather suffer than revenge:

and is so far from exacting the utmost farthing, that it had rather lose, than seek its own violently.

As it acts freely, so zealously too; but it is always to do good, for it hurts nobody.

An universal enemy against discord, and a holy cement for mankind.

And lastly, it is love to God and the brethren, which raises the soul above all worldly considerations: and as it gives a taste of heaven upon earth, so it is heaven, in the fulness of it, to the truly charitable here.

This is the noblest sense charity has: after which all should press, as that "more excellent way."

Nay, most excellent; for as faith, hope, and charity, were the more excellent way that the great apostle discovered to the Christians; (too apt to stick in outward gifts and church performances) so, of that better way, he preferred charity as the best part, because it would outlast the rest and abide forever.

Wherefore a man can never be a true and good Christian without charity, even in the lowest sense of it; and yet he may have that part thereof, and still be none of the apostle's true Christian: since he tells us, "That though we should give all our goods to the poor, and want charity, (in her other and higher senses) it would profit us nothing."

Nay, "though we had all tongues, all knowledge, and even gifts of prophecy, and were preachers to others, aye, and had zeal enough to give our bodies to be burned; yet if we wanted charity, it would not avail us for salvation.

It seems it was his (and indeed ought to be our) "Unum necessarium," or the "One thing needful;" which our Saviour attributed to Mary, in preference to her sister Martha, that seems not to have wanted the lesser parts of charity.

Would to God this divine virtue were more implanted and diffused among mankind, the pretenders to Christianity especially; and we should certainly mind piety more than controversy; and exercise love and compassion, instead of censuring and persecuting one another, in any manner whatsoever.